Spirit Guides:
ICONOCLAST

Questions with Answers
Through Trance Mediumship

*To You With Love
-From Us*

REV LYN GIBB DE SWARTE

Spirit Guides:
Iconoclast

Questions and Answers
Through Trance Mediumship

To You With Love From Us

Rev Lyn Gibb de Swarte

Copyright © 2021 by Rev Lyn Gibb de Swarte

All rights reserved. No part of this publication may be reproduced, distributed, or transmitted in any form or by any means, including photocopying, recording, or other electronic or mechanical methods, without the prior written permission of the publisher, except in the case of brief quotations embodied in critical reviews and certain other non-commercial uses permitted by copyright law.

ISBN-13: 979-8-50-902381-1

The moral rights of the author have been asserted.

Printed by: Kindle Direct Publishing

Published by:
The New Christian Spiritualists Society

Cover Design & Layout by:
Rev Nick Brown

Introduction

As we Spiritualists know, truth is stranger than fiction.

You will find wise and thought-provoking responses to some very pointed questions in this collection of spirit communication.

The fact is that there is a group of highly evolved beings who live in the realms of light, aka heaven, happy to communicate their collective knowledge to seekers after answers to a myriad of enquiries via their channel living here on the earth plane.

There are countless such groups on the spirit side of life as there always has been since humankind was placed on this planet, as there have been channels relaying their words.

And many of the spiritually engendered manuscripts that have been left to us by scribes from the beginning of recorded time.

But the selection you can access here were first written down and published in a Spiritualist newspaper in 1999.

Psychic News was a weekly Spiritualist newspaper that was first published in May 1932.

Its founding publisher and editor was trance medium and journalist Maurice Barbanell.

The spokesperson for the group in spirit for whom Maurice was the medium called himself Silver Birch.

The group told the earthly instrument for their communications that they wanted him to promote their teachings within the pages of his newspaper.

Now printed periodicals were the main sources of general information at that time and continued to be influential until more wireless receivers became part of general pre-war and wartime home life, and after that, television in the post-war early 1950's.

Even so, the companies that provided and controlled Britain's media maintained a perceivable upper and middle class, and establishmentarian, religious status quo, that did not admit of anything even vaguely Spiritualist.

In this 21st century the mainstream broadcasting channel programmers still studiously avoid serious Spiritualist content, although there are plenty of social media and online inroads being made by Spiritualist organisations, groups, individuals and churches.

Back in 1996 a new editor was appointed to Psychic News who was also a trance medium who worked with a group in spirit.

The group talked about the teachings of Silver Birch having been printed in the paper, and thereafter being collected into some volumes, and suggested they have some space in the same way.

After settling into the job, the editor agreed to enter a trance state once a week, in the office, and receive answers to questions that would be put by the assistant editor Cathy Gibb, now Gibb de Swarte, who would also act as scribe.

Then it was the turn of the medium having eventually agreed to their plan, to ask the group a question. You will have to give a name for the group. People need a name to relate to. After some discussion, basically a lecture on names and personalities, they agreed and pronounced, Iconoclast.

And on January 8th 1999 began the sessions that you can access within the pages of this book.

No intention to emulate the previous editor's action by publishing a volume thereafter was mooted.

However, a CD was made at their instigation, with fresh questions asked and some meditations given, in the trance state, that has proved quite popular since, and that was that.

Not quite! In 2021, in one of those inexplicable strange ways that we know Spirit works, access to some old copies of PN suddenly turned up containing those printed questions and answers, and that is how this compendium came into earthly circulation.

I trust that you will find them informative, uplifting and full of unconditional love and light and truth,
Rev Lyn Gibb de Swarte

May 2021

Principal Minister, The New Christian Spiritualists Society

January 8th, 1999

Can you tell us, What is your Mission?

Our mission is to bring light to this world of darkness to you who think that you live in the light, because you see the sunrise in the mornings and watch it descend toward your horizon in the evening.

You see the moon sail across your night sky, and you think that you see and live in the light but must know that this is but an illusion.

We wish to brighten your darkness, your spiritual darkness, with the light that comes from the Great Source of the only light there is.

We come to spread knowledge of the light which really shines only through the Great Spirit into your own, and thus you alone make the illumination in your world.

We do not deny your efforts on our behalf, but we must make more inhabitants of your world aware of their duty to spread the word of the One Alone who brings the light.

We desire no obeisance to ourselves because we, too are servants of the light. We do not sit in some authority over you.

We are the same as you but a little more enlightened at the time whereby we speak with you.

We only request that you understand that yourselves make the darkness of your world, and we would desire that you who are aware of the great gift of light, will work even harder to spread the word and thereby lighten your darkness.

We convey our love to all who work towards the light and the furtherance of the work which has yet to be fulfilled on earth.

May you live in peace.

"We wish to brighten your darkness, your spiritual darkness, with the light that comes from the Great Source of the only light there is..."

May 8 1999

Are you happy with the way Spiritualism is going at this moment in time?

Spiritualism is a concept of an almost unattainable ideal. However, there are those who say that they wish to be considered Spiritualists in a spiritual manner of thought and demonstrate to others that this is the way forward for all life.

Still, as in every grouping, there are among its number those who are what we may opine to be not particularly spiritual in their attitude of lifestyle.

Nor in reality, would they be Spiritualists except by their own definition. Spiritualism is a way of life that is life expressed in the highest motivational terms.

We have heard many millions affirm their belief in the ideas which are Spiritualist, but who come from many other belief systems. Over the millennia, there have lived many of those who have to bring the truths and truth of Spiritualism to the world.

There have been, shall we say, unfortunate consequences, and yet we who have seen so much disappointment in our communal cause have eternal hope, and whatever transpired before can only improve.

We take this opportunity to offer our love and encouragement to those who carry the burden that we once knew.

We wish to extend our thanks to those of you who understand this small communication for keeping the flame of human hope, for all that is good, burning brightly in what for you are sometimes almost incomprehensible earthly situations.

We give you hope.

"Over the millennia, there have lived many of those who have to bring the truths and truth of Spiritualism to the world..."

May 15 1999

Is there forgiveness for everyone in the Spirit world?'

As there are none who are born to the earth plane who are free from guilt, there is every need to enquire about the possibility of being forgiven for whatever it is that one would need forgiving for. Orthodox religion has always had its best customers from those who feel they need forgiving the most.

Unfortunately, the level of guilt suffered has no bearing on the crime that is supposed to have been committed. It is all a matter of personal conscience and of course how the being on the earth has been conditioned from birth by the adults responsible for its well being.

Where there is only love, forgiveness is not an issue. All is forgiven because everything is known and therefore everything is understood.

There is no penal system in heaven, and yes, there are places that seem to have no light in the world of Spirit, and yet light is everywhere and as some poor soul comes over and feels the weight and burden of wrongdoing upon them and their spirit, so the soul struggles and so progress is initiated, and so the pathway to the light and forgiveness is made clear.

The day of judgement is every day for all of us for this is the way of love and truth. And so all souls will attain the light eventually.

Out of bad always comes good. Love is all that is needed.

Love is.

"Where there is only love, forgiveness is not an issue. All is forgiven because everything is known and therefore everything is understood..."

May 22 1999

Will there be a solution and an end to the Kosovo war?

There is a solution, and an end is in sight for this particular sad and poor state of affairs in that part of the world today.

The solution has always been obvious unfortunately it does not suit the earthly powers that govern the world to implement that. The political situation in the Balkan area of Europe has always been volatile as is very well known.

It is an area full of different tribes of people who are just not interested in compromise, that which would have ever provided a solution.

The religious propensities of each tribe precluding them from the ability to interact with each other to everyone's detriment. In recent years there has been an awareness by all who study political science of this, what has become an eventuality.

No steps no appropriate moves were taken to prevent this current conflict which was only too obvious to those who watched silently from the sidelines and did nothing to avert catastrophe.

We who grieve for the ills of the earth are attempting to shed light into the souls of those responsible, and we are not referring to those combatants alone.

As before so the future unfolds according to that which is undertaken by humankind and therefore, we can say that in spite of all, that good and the right will prevail.

The truth must be served however unpleasant is the telling.

Those who live by the sword shall pass by the sword those who live by love shall experience the joy of love and must try to spread the love that they understand is the motivating force of all creation. They will prevail.

There will be hope for better things to come from those in high places of government.

Change is to come.

May God bless you all.

May 29 1999

Will there be a revival of the Lyceum Movement within Spiritualism?

There are many forces that are acting in contradictory fashion in respect of this rather knotty problem. There have been many attempts to restore faith in what after all is a worthy learning process.

You see there was a time when it was customary for the young of many families to take the opportunity that was offered in the tradition of the Sabbath School system that was used as a supplementary form of education in the underprivileged classes, we speak here of the British Isles.

There is not now such an interest taken by the majority of families now, although they now enjoy a greater material comfort in their lives.

In order to attract those who wish to learn the very basic principles of the Spiritualist way of life and religion it must be made more interesting and entertaining and accessible.

Echoing halls, however one tries to make them welcoming, lack a homely atmosphere and welcome. We do not mean to criticise the efforts of so many good souls, but we must say that change and modernisation of concept, must take place.

Where there are Spiritualist churches, centres and groups, this is where the Lyceum Movement, so beloved and necessary to the pioneers of Spiritualism, this wonderful way of life and religion, should flourish. There must be facilities offered for such learning.

It is fashionable now to include the mature student, but while you are attracting the mature student you will put off and not attend to the needs of the young and they are our future.

We are all guardians of that golden chain of spirit and knowledge, but we cannot impart wisdom by the same channels. We ask that those who differ in their approach to the question of revival should contrive first to inspire themselves and others to work together in at least some kind of harmony.

We are not suggesting a big dipper style of theme park or even a zoo in order to make a school for Spiritualism for the young more attractive, but at least something in the way of games, computer games, some healthy pursuits too, some outdoor fun and pets corner.

These things can be useful when considering a large centre, but we reiterate it is best to have local involvement. There are many good things about the old ways that can be useful and brought forward by modern invention.

There will continue to be much argument and debate for some time to come, but in time there will be a new movement for the Lyceum.

Education is the key.

June 6 1999

Why is it that in this way of life, when you have proof of life after death and experience, that a shock or sudden death can be so difficult to get over?

The words that you have chosen with which to couch your question must give you the clue to its answer.

Shock, trauma, unexpectedness by those on the earth plane is the cause of so much discomfort and upset.

The elevation - for that is what it mostly is - of the spirit in leaving the physical body is not always appreciated by those still inhabiting the same.

Those who are left to carry on with their earthly lives and particularly those who shoulder great burdens, sometimes alone, as a result of a passing to spirit, find their path ahead sometimes too dreadful to contemplate.

So you see that the problems of bereavement are many and various, and when this situation occurs without warning, it is made even worse. We who welcome your loved ones into our domain would hope that the knowledge of an eternal life, a never-ending flame of spirit would sustain and comfort you.

While there are negative impulses around those left behind at such times, the positive awareness of that one who has passed so shockingly must be made into a positive life course of action.

The fact that those called Spiritualists are positive in their trust that there is life after the material dies will be comforted, come what may, and will further understand that we are all with God.

The physical side of life is to be left to the physical if that is the need of the moment, but the spirit of each and every one of us is able to be touched, one to the other, and so on, and in this way we soothe and pacify the wounded.

June 12 1999

Would Maurice Barbanell like to contribute something to Psychic News?

Maurice Barbanell has never ceased to have an influence on the Psychic News. It may be that he has a little more input now than he has previously enjoyed since his passing to the spirit world.

He is occasionally not impressed with some of the correspondence that the present Editor has to endure. He would not have had as much patience as she.

He had little time for the foolish, in his opinion of course, but plenty for those who were, and are perceived to be, of a decent intellectual quality of mind, and mediumistic ability.

He has made his presence felt more than once in the offices of Psychic News. He has been well received by the present Editor.

There are many problems that seem to be never ending, just like life itself, for the paper which we at the time, brought into being.

We would like to see more editorial all round. We would appreciate a little more support from all concerned, for the efforts that are being made in the Editorial seat.

Maurice Barbanell sends his greetings from this world to the other. You may work out from your own viewpoint which one is which.

What are your beliefs on Reincarnation?

You are addressing a group in the world of spirit as though they were one person. This is in error. We who work together have spoken many times before on this subject.

We are not of the opinion that it serves the greater purpose, by dwelling on matters which divide, rather than bring together, those who deign to call themselves Spiritualists, as which many of our number would be known before our passing.

There are times when a single spirit may choose, or be directed, to return to the earth plane in order to serve the Great Creator, and this is chronicled in earth history.

But for the most part, those like ourselves who have served our time on the earth plane, remain in spirit only, until such time as the Great Spirit may decide otherwise.

There are some of our number who are not yet acquainted with the physical morass on the earth, but we must say that so far in the light of their own knowledge, they have expressed the thought that they do not feel that they have missed very much.

We who are companions in spirit here, are happy that you have spoken with us today, and we wish you God speed, as we return to the etheric realm.

May the Great Spirit bless all who peruse the pages of what is, after all, our own periodical.

July 3 1999

Is Arthur Findlay buried at the local Stansted church and why?

Is he happy with the way Spiritualism is now going and did he foresee that his Stansted home would also be extended into a healing centre namely the Pioneers Centre?

First of all it is not of any importance to the world of spirit where, what, or how, physical remains are disposed of, neither where they may or may not lay.

We remind you that the spirit is everything and the physical is purely a temporary temporal adjunct while we understand the need for some to hold on to the physicality of one or many of those who have preceded them into the spirit realms.

Arthur Findlay conveys congratulations to those who keep the torch of knowledge still burning brightly and in the face of what is still somewhat overwhelming opposition to the truths of Spiritualism, but he is pleased that those whose avowed way of life is guided by spirit and that within Spiritualism are moving in a positive direction, and with education much in the forefront of their minds, removing the curse of ignorance.

As for whether Arthur Findlay foresaw the extension of his College for the Advancement of Psychic Science.

We would say yes, and that healing was a very good means by which to attract more people into our way of life which of course was his.

The Pioneers Centre is aptly named, and one which he would have chosen himself if he had been asked at the time.

The Centre itself was named through inspiration from spirit as was the entire project.

We wish to make it clear that all such healing centres and places where healing through Spiritualist ministration is offered are all as equally important to us and there is nowhere that Spiritualist healing takes place that is not dear to us.

God Bless You All!

July 10 1999

Is Spiritualism an exclusive club?

It is true that some of those who call themselves Spiritualists consider, or appear to be convinced, that that is the case.

They tend to form themselves into coteries for the purpose of pursuing their avowed philosophical religious and scientific belief system, and ensure by their behaviour and demeanour, that those they may not wish to associate themselves with, are not made to feel able to apply for membership.

Many seem to operate along the lines of the old gentlemen's clubs including golf clubs, and of course topically for the sunshine months Lords, the Marylebone Cricket Club of course based at the Lords ground, they try to influence those around them into adopting this same exclusivity, and by so doing stunt their spiritual growth.

Spiritualism is indeed a universal truth, unfortunately just like any other truth it can become distorted in the telling. There are many different ways of expressing spirituality, and spirit, that exists within the nomenclature, Spiritualism.

In the British Isles there are many different groups, and we give them the same weight of our love and thought and understanding.

By the same token, there are groups of spiritual people outside of that fine web of light that encapsulates Spiritualism. These are the various religions, and we must include the earth religions, as well as those who look towards the space without.

We have a special caring for those within rigid belief systems, and we would like to see more of those followers of perhaps great masters who have visited the earth, to be accepted into Spiritualist enclaves, in order for Spiritualism to extend, and extend into the consciousness of those who at present are unaware of the truth, that we are all one.

Spiritualism as a world and universal philosophy cannot be considered as the exclusive domain of any one being or group of beings, before God. Spiritualism will prevail for the people.

There will be no end. All and everything is under God's protection.

No membership cards are needed.

July 17 1999

Should Spiritualists participate in the Millennium Celebrations?

Spiritualism is the celebration of all life, therefore it is fitting that those who consider themselves to be Spiritualists should participate in any celebration of life, whomsoever calls together such a gathering for its purpose; whether or not we celebrate any one life enhancing event or another, makes no difference to the intention that owes so much to the wish to do good for one's fellow creatures.

A birthday of course is a cause for delight amongst those who welcome a new being into the earth plane no matter whose advent it might be; but of course it would be foolish to ignore the fact that the commonly used world calendar uses the assumed birth date of the great teacher Jesus or Yeshua of Nazareth as he is known.

There is no reason in heaven or earth that we can think of, and we think of a great deal, that would preclude the celebration of the 2,000 year anniversary of that birth.

Many understand that individual dates of entry into the physical incarnation by spirit is sometimes a haphazard affair of record.

In some cultures such a record is not kept according to the day and date and time, but is approximated to a religious festival time, in this case we can look at the most appropriate festival of lights, always around December time.

It is appropriate for those who come within the remit of Spiritualism and its philosophy of all embracing love to take this opportunity which is only the second time a century has been marked for modern Spiritualists, and the very first time that those who call themselves Spiritualists are to celebrate the counting of a New Millennium, and can thus demonstrate a new way of living life, a new kind of spiritual awareness, to so many other spiritually motivated groups, such as those for whom the Millennium is so significant to their beliefs.

We will be there with our love and undying support.

July 25 1999

What are the group's views on abortion, and do foetuses grow and develop as human beings in the spirit world?

Those of our number who were once incarnate on the earth plane, have perhaps a more practically based understanding of this problem.

We understand that the term abortion, is applied to that, which is in our opinion, an offence against another physical being by another.

However, given the difficulties that abound in the material world, we temper our conviction. with the mercy with which the love of God operates, and it is beholden upon us to minister with such grace.

There are times when abortion is known, by those in the world of spirit, in advance, and in those cases certain pre-emptive measures and decisions are taken. This applies to the spirit being who will experience the physical for such a short time.

Such tragedies, for in all creation, life that is ended by all expectation too soon, is always regarded as such, but they have been, since the beginning of time. On the other hand, we accept mitigating circumstances, and it is these circumstances that lend themselves to the greater purpose.

There is as every aware being knows, a need to learn through suffering. Unfortunately it has often been said that the strongest steel is forged in the hottest furnace, and so it is with the human spirit. Now as for that spirit which is within the unborn being, there are on occasion old spirit beings, who have no need to visit the earth plane yet again and who volunteer, if you can call anything that we who do God's bidding, volunteering, to occupy the physical mass for a little while, in order to serve a greater purpose, perhaps the further education of all those concerned.

For the most part. the new spirit that has to return after a microcosmic stay in earthly time, matures as a whole being, but not at the same rate as if that growth were measured in earth years, and without the accompanying physical trauma

There are many brothers and sisters of those now dwelling in the earth plane, in the world of spirit, and who they have never met. Although this may cause some problem to those who have experienced abortion, we would comfort them with the knowledge that all in the higher realms of spirit is pure love, care and devotion, to the Great Creator. We do not sit in judgement on those who are still attempting to find their way through their earthly life, but send our compassion that one day we trust will pervade the earth plane and so be in heaven and earth the same.

July 25 1999

Are there such things as Aliens who visit the Earth Plane? If so, where do they come from? And could they come from the world of Spirit?

There are of course no aliens as we are all brothers and sisters in spirit, whether we inhabit one bodily form or another while in the physical world it makes no difference to the essential truth that all under God are as one.

There is constant visitation as all who know the truth know by those of us who inhabit the realms of light alone. We are all held in this web of eternal light both literal and figurative.

Since the beginning of time the human being has suspected his and her neighbour, of at the very least, wanting something from them, and at the very worst, desiring to murder them, usually for materialistic gain but unfortunately also for some perceived a-physical motive.

The concept of cannibalism being one that is one of the most base of human animal instincts.

The fear of being controlled by someone or something that has a greater power than our own, is one that needs to be overcome, and in the pursuit of knowledge of the spiritual kind we must relinquish this fear, and give full control in our lives to God. There are those who in their physical incarnation were never of the planet earth, but from places far distant, but they are not alien beings, they are the same as you now, and as we were, and are.

We bring you greetings from those, who having shuffled off the mortal coil, are free to roam God's universe and all the cosmos. God bless you all!

"We are all held in this web of eternal light both literal and figurative..."

August 7 1999

Shall we be with those we love in the spirit world, although separated by convention in the physical world?

For those who have lived a good life, satisfaction for their spiritual self will follow after the transition called death.

This of course is not the same as physical gratification. If the love that is born to another, or others, on the physical plane whilst living here, is of a selfless and caring kind, then it shall be that there will be no division in the realm of light thereafter.

There is no easy answer for those who might be suffering the pain of separation from those they love in the physical world as a result of misunderstandings or even what is sometimes termed a pigheadedness on the part of either party to such upsetting situations, but as we pass into the realm of light where all are asked to consider their actions and the subsequent reactions upon both themselves and others, so enlightenment, forgiveness, and caring, heal the breaches made whilst living on the earth plane.

There have been many happy reunions, when those who have been separated by various circumstances but who do indeed have a love for each other, soon after passing over themselves.

When we live on the earth plane in the grosser material of the physical world there is much to be learned, and the pain of separation from loved ones is the most hard in our opinion, thus we comfort those who suffer at the present time and assure them that all will be alright in the end.

God bless you all!

"There is no easy answer for those who might be suffering the pain of separation from those they love in the physical..."

August 14 1999

What would have been the reaction of Charles Dickens and H.G. Wells, who were anti-Spiritualist and lifelong rationalists, when they passed on and found themselves in a spirit world in which they do not believe?

Just like many others of their contemporaries, H.G. and his associates of like mind, were the proverbial ostriches, burying their heads in the sand of materialism, masquerading as rationalism, who on viewing giraffes for the first time brought to the London Zoo, exclaimed, "I do not believe it!" Nevertheless, imaginative persons such as Mr Wells, indulged in flights of fancy, that have rarely been equalled, by those of us contemporary at that time on the earth plane, that we who were pleased to admit of the truth of Spiritualism would have been loath to own up to.

We would go so far as to say that this gentleman author and deep thinker would have had more than an inkling of spirit assistance in his professional life.

Indeed, Charles Dickens admitted that in fact he envisaged all his stories and the characters therein as though acting out a play before his very eyes, and almost all he had to do was to write a description of what he heard and saw.

There is no doubt for those who follow the facts of Spiritualist thought that those described as geniuses in their field were also mediums for communication from the world of spirit.

You may like to consider such as Mr Gilbert and Mr Sullivan and their artistic outpourings as well as the pleasure that their musing brought to those on the earth plane, whose darkness they were all lightening.

If those now of an interested disposition should read Mr Wells' works, they will be made only too aware that what we have said is the truth.

The gift of seeing further than the ordinary level enjoyed by those dwelling on the earth plane is called commonly clairvoyance. There was no shock to Mr Wells when he awoke to find himself dead, anymore there was for Mr Dickens, although one was so covert about his own greater knowledge.

Many are life's circumstances that dictate whether or not we possess a belief which seems contrary to common thinking, just as much now for many, almost as there was then.

Neither will there be any shocks on finding themselves still conscious individuals inhabiting these realms by many claiming disbelief and so-called rational argument at this present time.

We are glad that you asked this question and all of us send greetings particularly from erstwhile so-called rationalists who are of our number.

May the sun always shine upon you all as the light of creation shines in your world and in ours.

August 21 1999

If animals, not pets, do not survive individually, what relationship exists between the Great Spirit and an uncared-for or ill-treated animal?

How does the life of such an animal reveal the love of Justice of the Great Spirit, viewing it as a matter between the Creator and the created?'

Does the questioner ask if animals survive in spirit?

How arrogant and ill-considered such a question is. The animal kingdom is represented in the realms of spirit in much the same way as it is represented during the earthly lifetimes of its denizens while they are on the earth plane.

There is no amorphous blob to which animals belong. It is sheer effrontery and egoism on the part of some human beings to so denigrate those of their brethren in spirit as to allow for such base imaginings.

All living things have their place in the universe and therefore in the grander scheme of eternity. Animals do not require the love of human beings to sustain their spirit, although care should be taken to ensure their physical survival on the earth.

This has been thankfully more prevalent of latter years.

Psychic News has been in the forefront of the spreading of such information as is needed to promote animal welfare.

It certainly is a matter of utmost importance to the created by the Creator, in as much as the human must deal justly, on behalf of that which created them, towards the animal kingdom.

When human beings who were also created by the same Creator, behave in a principled, and just and holy way, toward the rest of creation in its entirety, so shall justice be done.

Amen.

We wish to enlighten and not admonish. We ask that humankind actively seek to better the lot of their fellow creatures over whom they were given responsibility.

May universal love prevail.

September 4 1999

Can you tell us the manner in which power is created on your side of life, that is, the power that is characterised for particular conditions with people who are ill?

That which is referred to as power that is somehow created on the spirit side of life, is an eternal force generated by good for good.

There is no special aspect of that eternal creation, that constant source of energy, that is necessary to be made in any way different when used by, if you like, microcosmic particles of that same divine energy, to effect healing for those who are sick in any way on the earth plane.

It is those small instruments of the Almighty who may alter in some way to do the most good, and that is where we are, within the power of good. What makes one person a better healer than another?

We think that we have already touched on that subject. You know that there are many different kinds of characteristics in any one human being, countless facets of the one, and all these are contributory factors that affect healing that is given.

You see the power is universal and envelops all, but that power, which is of spirit, and not of physical matter, the common sense of those words, is also diverse in its wholeness. Those who would exercise their healing gifts from the spirit side of life, prefer to work with what they personally consider to be suitable mediums for their work.

We will not speak here of earthly sacrifice, of the subjugation of the baser motivations of human beings, nor too much of expectation of spiritual attainment while still on the earth plane and pursuing earthly business, but we will reiterate that as you think, so shall you attract.

May the healing power of God's universe be with you!

September 11 1999

What is Alzheimer's? Do you have any comfort for those who are suffering with it, and those who are caring for people with the disease?

This is one of the causes of that which is collectively known as dementia. This is named after the discoverer and describes a physical condition of a degenerative nature which afflicts the brain and the nature of which is being researched by those persons of science on the earth plane at the present time.

We are mindful of the agonies that this dreadful disease causes to both the sufferer and those who care for them. Nevertheless, we reiterate that the mind is not the brain, the brain generates impulses across the network housed within the skull the faculties of memory and learning which are so important to the mental wellbeing of the person who is the receptor of these faculties.

There is much work on genetic modification being undertaken at this time and so far it has only resulted in cleverer mice. While we applaud the preservation of the physical abilities to understand and benefit from the physical environment, we have misgivings about the ultimate objectives of such engineering work.

We can only join with you in the hope that those who are now suffering and who will suffer in the near future with this disabling disease shall be relieved by medication of their torment and that in the future this disease will not hold human beings anymore in its vicious grip.

But again we say that the mind which resides within the etheric body is like the spirit self, intact and unflawed by physical disability and disease, and it is possible to have communication with the mind of that spirit within, that we all are, and of which we are all a part.

We must remember that we are part of the eternal song of the universe and we say to you remember the words of the servant of God, the Lord God is my shepherd I shall not want and so we shall all lie down in pastures green by the still waters and we shall all dwell in the house of God for ever more.

May you and yours feel to be at peace and at one with God.

September 18 1999

How would you explain the Great Spirit to children?

Little children could be said to live in a state of grace owing to their proximity to the source of their life.

They have as newly incarnated spirit to the earth plane an innocent and happy acceptance of the life in the physical sense that they feel themselves to be participants in as children grow older in conscious earth years, so they begin to question both how they came to be born here and the bigger question that remains with them until they eventually reclaim that spirit land from whence they came, why they are here.

This searching for that answer should result at least in an inkling of an omnipresent and omniscient source of life.

It has been very difficult to separate the images that have been made of that source which are invariably physical depictions of men, women, birds and beasts from the reality as we and those of you who are so enlightened know to be a lake of love and light, the truth, and how can we tell children what love, light and truth looks like.

It has always been easier to refer to a God who looks like any other human being, and in most cases, is a representative of just a section of humanity. We who are of spirit alone have no colour, hair type and dare we say, gender, although we have the experience and knowledge that our physical lives afforded us in our eternal progress.

Better to tell our children of the earth that they are children of the light of love and truth absolute, and that this Great Spirit is all pervading of themselves, ourselves, yourselves and is all around outside too.

If children have this fact explained to them, after their first forgetting, this world in which they dwell will deal more kindly with all of them until their ultimate return, so that the children shall suffer not.

Amen.

October 2 1999

Is there forgiveness in the Spirit World?

As there are none who are born to the earth plane who are free from guilt, there is every need to enquire about the possibility of being forgiven for whatever it is that one would need forgiving for.

Orthodox religion has always had its best customers from those who feel they need forgiving the most. Unfortunately, the level of guilt suffered has no bearing on the crime that is supposed to have been committed.

It is all a matter of personal conscience and of course how the being on the earth has been conditioned from birth by the adults responsible for its well-being.

Where there is only love, forgiveness is not an issue. All is forgiven because everything is known and therefore everything is understood.

There is no penal system in heaven, and yes, there are places that seem to have no light in the world of Spirit, and yet light is everywhere and as some poor soul comes over and feels the weight and burden of wrongdoing upon them and their spirit, so the soul struggles and so progress is initiated, and so the pathway to the light and forgiveness is made clear.

The day of judgement is every day for all of us for this is the way of love and truth.

And so all souls will attain the light eventually.

Out of bad always comes good. Love is all that is needed.

Love is.

"Where there is only love, forgiveness is not an issue. All is forgiven because everything is known and therefore everything is understood..."

October 9 1999

Is there a lot of truth in the Bible?

You know the expression where there is smoke there must be fire, in much the same way this selection of books that were put together by, we hasten to add many, contains much that is true, but it would pay to be selective.

The truth has for all time stood and will continue with or without the Bible that some call holy.

There is much historical content within the ancient writings. It is not necessary to dwell on such well-known truths as the flood as there is a wealth of corroborative evidence to support what might otherwise be called a figment of someone's imagination. There was a flood, that is the truth.

What is not the truth is that it was caused by the Great Spirit. It was an ecological disaster caused by severe climatic changes at that time.

The man Moses did climb the mountain and he did hear from us at that time; that is the truth. We sought to bring some order into the lives of those living on the earth plane in rather dire circumstances at that time; that is the truth.

What is not the truth is that the Great Spirit spoke those words. We will not at this time say too much about events that led to the compilation of more recent writings about the one they call Jesus.

When those engaged in pursuing spiritual discourse become emotionally involved as they tend to do it affects their judgement; this is the truth.

Yes, there is truth in the biblical accounts of life in those far off days, but it is tempered with the minds of men who also walked the earth a long time ago.

What every individual who seeks the truth must do is, without emotional entanglement, assess the facts laid before them in the light of their own knowledge and that of others whose deliberations do not assault their reason.

The truth is.

Oct 16 1999

Will Spiritualism Ever Become A Universal Religion?

Ever is a long time and the answer must be an emphatic yes. So far it has only been acknowledged for just over one century and a half, so if you wish to compare that time scale to that of other more established belief systems which have been around the earth plane for thousands of earth years, you will understand that Spiritualism as a universal concept is in its extreme infancy.

Those who work for Spiritualism on the spirit side of life are concerned that there should be sustained effort made by more than just in comparative terms a few dedicated to the task of spreading the truth.

Spiritualism is mostly made up of the word spiritual, although some would say that this is perhaps not a fair description or connotation of the inner concept of what Spiritualism is all about.

There are many who could be called spiritual, many millions, or who could be said to possess spirituality.

However, the reality is that those two words do not add up to Spiritualism. Spiritualism is not just founded on communication between the physical earthly dimension and others.

It is also the way in which the knowledge of eternal life, is put to use. There are naturally many aspects of Spiritualist philosophy that stems from that original vantage point of knowledge, that are to be found in almost every other world religion, but they do not only have just fragments of Spiritualist truth, but these are augmented with other baser trappings and accoutrements.

The human being desires ceremonial, desires tangible manifestation of spiritual truth. Spiritualism preaches the truth that is found in the harmonious order of life and life eternal.

We say again that truth is to be found by those who seek all around in creation, and the light of truth shines for those who would see it with a perception unrelated to the physical.

All creation, and beings within that creation, are of immeasurable value to the Great Spirit to whom they are always connected, but we who have an overview look forward to the time when indeed the truth in Spiritualism will be universal, and the divisive sectarianism of being from being will cease.

Spiritualists, those who accept that Spiritualism is the only rational philosophy for life, must continue to press on with our mission. May peace prevail on earth.

Oct 23 1999

How are we to express the displeasure of the majority towards evil doers in our midst, and mete out reprimand within a Spiritualistic understanding? In Teheran, three convicted of murder are to be executed, and one convicted of being their 'look out' man, blinded.

Although people complain often that Spiritualism has not 'done much' to obviously change the world order in the 151 years since its inception - just think of the spirit impulses that have been at work in that short time.

Slavery came to an end. Markedly in America, which became a united body of previously disaffected and often warring states, as well as in other parts of the world. Instruments of torture are now no longer in evidence in prisons in the Western world where Spiritualism has taken firm root.

Women also are considered differently from that categorisation from which they suffered up to the middle of the last century.

They are now restored to equality in the areas affected by knowledge of Spiritualism.

Since the advent of Spiritualism, earthly science has moved on apace. Magic carpets, made of metal fly not just around the world but out to the moon and planets beyond, and medicine and surgical practice is unrecognisable from that of the mid 19th century.

The truths of Spiritualism are working through its adherents and the good workers for the Great Spirit are spreading those principles.

As they impinge on the consciousness of those around them, so the influence of what used to be termed 'holy spirit' is felt, and here and there acted upon. Thus producing the progress that has been recorded so far.

In the matter of punitive measures taken against weak-spirited brethren by those for whom Spiritualism is presently a closed book, those who are blessed with awareness, must continue to strive in a positive and non-aggressive manner, through social means, to take the message of Spiritualism - primarily one of love and service - out to all.

Love is blind - it does not seek to blind, either spiritually or physically. Service is the essence of life and seeks only to enhance and preserve that essence in others. It does not kill.

Spiritualist education is the key to a better way of life for everyone and is the way in which a Spiritualist justice system would operate.

The eternal progress open to every human soul must be initiated from the earth plane in this practical application.

Oct 30 1999

Please can you tell me when we pass to spirit, is it possible to travel the world and to see all the wonderful and exotic places that ordinary people are unable to see because of lack of money while on this earth?

The short answer is yes. Naturally, the spirit when it is freed from the earthly shackles does indeed fly to dwell in the spirit realms in special conjunction with God, the Great Spirit itself.

This is the freedom that is so often spoken of in ancient scriptures. The freedom to traverse not only the world from which you came but all others.

The lack of material substance in the life everlasting is a positive attribute, not like the miserable existence it affords one when dwelling on the earth plane, without the millstones of property whether it be of bricks and mortar, livestock or jewels, one attains the wealth and riches of the spirit untrammelled by earthly material and physical considerations.

There are avenues to be explored for such exotic excursions that can take place without money while you are still on the earth plane and still in the physical body by joining in a meditation class guided by good spirit teachers where you will find yourself taken on many a wonderful trip. There are many beauties to be seen with the inner spirit eye such as warm sands and sea and palm trees, oases in the deserts, mountain tops to be scaled, icy rivers to glide over, crystal caves to wander through and libraries full of every book, every manuscript that has ever been written, all these things and yes even an occasional voyage to the stars can be yours through such a channel.

When the material life is over, so the spirit may, according to the way in which one has lived one's life, enjoy the next stage in its evolution and progress. For many this begins in beautiful gardens along with their loved ones who have gone before, but we caution against hastening that time artificially.

We wish you all a good life here and in the hereafter.

Nov 6 1999

Is it necessary to live a spiritual life in order to become a good medium?

It has been shown that it is not necessary to have previously lived a spiritual life to change direction at any one time and taking positive steps to become more spiritual. If that were the case then there would have been very few instances of mediumship over the last few millennia.

Even those held in reverence in the old scriptures had not led by any means blameless lives prior to them taking up the call to become a medium to the world of spirit, and it goes without saying, of God.

That does not mean that a spiritual life is not to be searched for striven for and being of benefit to the individual as well as the world around them into which they come into contact.

A spiritual nature is sometimes considered to be of a somewhat boring quality, however, it is better to be thought a little dull than to be considered among your brethren wicked and interesting.

Mediumship is by its very delineation a sacred task and whatever the faults, the errors and the mistakes of the past, if these are truly regretted and a new path carved out of what was previously nothing but barren and rocky hillside it is all the more commendable, for there can be a greater understanding of the way of the world and others' needs. When it comes to levels of mediumship, then spiritual awareness, and the spirituality of the one who would be the interlocutor between this world and the other world, it is good to have access on both sides to the highest minds' communication.

There is much enjoyment, interest and matters fascinating to be found in a spiritual lifestyle especially for those who would be mediums.

May you always be aware of spirit and the truth.

Nov 13 1999

Do you regard hypnotism as a short cut to spiritual development?

There is no short cut to spiritual development. There have been many attempts to produce quick results in the field of psychism which is a different thing. Spiritual development rests on the conscience of the individual and on the collective mind set.

To attain a spirituality in its higher forms, much thought and work needs to be applied, in no small part to the ingesting of information concerning spiritual matters as a proper regime, through that which may be spoken written or shown in any way.

It is also dependent on the way in which life's experiences are applied to the present time. That the spiritual truth-seeking individual finds themselves altering state of brain impulses in order to influence the mind consciousness is something that is inherently practised by all who seek to bridge the divide between the world of matter and the realms of spirit life.

This does not unfortunately have any bearing on the spiritual attainment of the would be exponent. There are of course many instances of valuable communication being allowed through the mesmeric influence.

It can also be said that a form of self-hypnosis takes place when the medium alters their own state of consciousness, sometimes with very extraordinary results in affecting physical matter in other ways as the brain pattern can be altered and the brain is a physical phenomenon, so it affects the mind which is of the spirit and the discarnate system.

The hypnotic state is also responsible when induced by outside will for communications of both a spiritual nature and that of which is not nice.

The road to spiritual development is a rocky one indeed and a long one.

May the Great Spirit walk with you on yours.

Nov 20 1999

Why do we ask God to forgive us our sins: for if the Law is broken does not the penalty follow?

Those who commit offences against humankind, animal kind, the planet on which they live, whether that be against an individual or any particular grouping, it is not the Great Spirit to whom they should address their requests for forgiveness, but to those against whom they have transgressed.

There is no forgiveness without reparation, restitution and the desire to make full compensation to whatever and whoever has been the victim of such offence. Even if one feels oneself to be forgiven of sin through whatever other means of supplication is employed, it should be accepted that this is a purely self-gratification situation which has no bearing on reality.

It is much easier for those who feel themselves weighed down by their own sinful behaviour to believe that they are forgiven by God through often self-appointed earthly intermediaries than to make what may have to be superhuman efforts to receive any small measure of ease of conscience from those or that which has been sinned against. Understanding ourselves and our motives and the circumstances which give rise to that which is considered sinful means that we are the first people from whom we have to seek that forgiveness from before we can imagine we are forgiven by the

Great Spirit, part of whom dwells within each and every one of us - all who are incarnate possess that divine spark. First, we must be able to forgive ourselves. If we cannot find a reason to forgive ourselves we must at least do whatever we can to alleviate suffering that we have caused without. Our inner suffering is part of that system of compensation and retribution that is part of the Spiritualist way of life.

This is the reality of sin and forgiveness thereafter. It is far better to make amends for that which we recognise as being wrongdoing whilst still living on the earth plane than to travel on to this next dimension of existence encumbered by guilt. It could be said that it does no harm to ask for forgiveness from God for if you perform a wrong act against any part of God's creation so you perform a wrong act against God who dwells within everything. But if in the asking you imagine forgiveness as your automatic right, then not only are you mistaken but condemned to have to consider your actions in the true light of God's love in the hereafter.

It may be that by this seemingly innocuous act of expunging guilt many will be made to feel better, but it is a spurious feeling and should be avoided for the greater good. Ask yourself at all times whether you forgive yourself your trespasses. At all times show the mercy unto others that you would wish shown to yourself. May God bless and keep you.

Nov 27 1999

We are told that God knows when a sparrow falls. How is it possible for God to know of all that happens to all the vast population of the world, not to mention the countless millions who have passed on?

God is the great all-pervading and encompassing without beginning nor end, Spirit. Everything that exists is a part of the infinite consciousness of everything which is God.

Suppose that you take as an example of God's situation as being your good self. If something happens to you, then you are aware of it. We are speaking here of your conscious self.

In the same way God knows all that happens to it. We know it is difficult to understand or accept God the Great Creator as neither possessing a physical substance shape or form to which the human being wishes to relate.

The Great Spirit is not constrained by physicality and is therefore neither male nor female nor both.

There have been a few over the ages since planet Earth came into being who have attempted to relay the message of such a God.

A God whose centre is everywhere and whose circumference is nowhere because the concept is too vast.

The scientists and mathematicians join now with the up to now perceived as only creative artists to present this possibility as a fact, that even a microcosmic point also contains planes.

All thinking humankind have always sought to find the whereabouts of God in their deliberations. They are fortunate who find God where they are.

God is truly everywhere, has always been and will always be, knowing everything, for everything is created by God.

As we know our own work so does God. Intervention, that is another matter.

God will bless you and keep you forever and ever.

Dec 4 1999

What advice can you give to anyone who wishes to start a home circle?

There are many kinds of home circles. So we will assume a generality of requirement. First of all, there must be a prevailing atmosphere of peace and contentment within.

It must be properly clean and the seating arranged to give comfort to those who will participate in any such circle, there need be no special paraphernalia in the room but be aware that material furnishings may fade a little, in the process of time.

It is necessary for there to be no interference from outside noise. Nor incursion from persons outside of the invited gathering. Those who wish to sit in a home circle will find out whether they are sitting with others who are of entirely like mind quite soon after any circle's commencement.

It is always hoped that those who wish to come together in the setting of a home circle shall be of common purpose and intent, but this may not prove to be the case.

It is not necessary to sit in dark and gloomy light levels, nor to light candles or use air fresheners such as incense or perfumes, although it is nice to have sweet fresh air in any enclosed space.

Loose comfortable clothing should be worn.

Definitely no tight garments or shoes or other footwear. This can play havoc with circle members' circulation and may cause some discomfort and swellings. We have always liked a potted plant or flower or two in any circle room but that is just a personal preference.

The circle leader must be competent in psychic and spiritual matters in their own right apart from having the ability to accept knowledge about any given eventuality or happening within such circles given from the spirit realms.

The leader if they are not a medium for spirit communication should ensure they have the services of such a one. It is an idea that where possible a record is kept of home circle work for the benefit of participants.

We in the spirit realms keep our own records. There are so many different reasons for instigating a home circle; such as that which sits for the development of one who would be a particular kind of medium or those which sit for the manifestation of physical phenomena.

We in the spirit realms see no end to our work in assisting wherever and whenever it is needed especially in the training grounds which are called home circles.

As long as the home circle is dedicated to the truth in light and love there can be no failure.

We wish all home circles Godspeed.

Dec 11 1999

There is a lot of controversy regarding reincarnation. Would it not be wiser to concern ourselves with survival?

The question of survival is paramount to Spiritualist belief. It is the knowledge that is imparted through that communication with the world of spirit in which we all survive which gives the proof that is needed to convince those who would otherwise live their earthly lives in ignorance of this fact.

Whether souls re-enter the fleshly coverings of the spirit in earthly guise, or whether they may not, is certainly nothing to do with providing evidence of survival.

There are many fascinating aspects to the concept of reincarnation by individual entities, some such as the prospect of belonging to a highly evolved group soul appeals to some, while others prefer to consider that only a part of their consciousness inhabits an earthly form at any one time and for any period of time.

There are those who prefer to consider themselves almost as prototypes. In other words, a one and only, if you like, manifestation of the Great Spirit, in some small part of course, while living out their allotted one life span.

There are as many ideas on reincarnation as there are followers of the idea. The only real difficulty is one of credibility when referring to what of necessity will always be viewed as a hypothesis which can never provide sufficient information to convince the sceptic of an after life.

To enable the truth about the human condition in particular to be expounded as an extension of an eternal life given to all, the concentration must be on that evidence of survival delivered through intermediary visionaries.

All the millions of people who have been incarnate on the planet Earth are all spirit too, have always been and will always be, and whether there is any toing and froing, we consider to be of no consequence in the argument for proving survival in the spirit world.

A lady has written to ask whether her dog is in the spirit world and will she see him again and we send her our reassurance that the answer to both questions is, 'Yes'.

Until we meet again.

Dec 18 1999

If a child dies as a result of an accident, was that intended by the Great Spirit?

There are many factors which are at work throughout someone's lifetime that determine when an individual shall pass back to the spirit world.

Accidents are by definition just that, unplanned for events.

All who are living on the physical earth plane owe their existence to the spirit that motivates them as individuals, however the ongoing interaction with other individuals and sentient beings, as well as the vegetable and mineral environment, all contribute to whether or not an accident will happen.

It is said accidents will happen and they do, with alarming regularity, as the sale of sticking plasters and soothing ointments for cuts and grazes will testify to.

The big accidents that cost the future life on earth of a small one are to be regretted by all who are concerned, but it is a fact of life itself, and it is not only impossible, but inadvisable, to be unduly mindful and watchful of the young, and preventing them from exploring their boundaries and physical possibilities that they encounter.

Even though such a departure from the earthly life may take place, it is a matter of fact that the young as well as the old inherit the kingdom of heaven, and it must be said that for some children, it is a beautiful awakening to a life such as they never knew before.

We do not suggest that you allow children to play with weapons or in such a manner or place that may harm themselves or each other, but if the worst in earthly terms befalls them, then they awake to the life eternal in all its splendour, and with those who love them in attendance, where there is no more hurt and no more accidents.

A life without accidents is only to be found in the glory of the spirit world. May their guardian angels continue to watch over every child as it is born onto the earth plane, that it may not suffer such accident.

Jan 01 2000

Is There As Much Of God In All Of Us As There Is Anywhere?

Anywhere is a very large place, but for the purpose of answering that question, we shall assume that your anywhere refers to anything in your known world apart from the human being.

It is because there is more of God as you put it, in the human being, that one is able to formulate such a question which would be beyond the capability of anything else anywhere else. The Great Spirit is indeed everywhere and anywhere, but the proportion of the God spirit differs when it comes to the human being.

This is where the human being, understanding this, instinctively made the decision for themselves that God made the human being in the likeness of itself - personified in the form of a man in the first instance.

This primitive concept is erroneous, nevertheless, a portion of the God spirit that is if you like the mind of God operates within the human being as a driving, reasoning, learning force, more than that to be found anywhere. It has become fashionable in these more egalitarian and socially conscious times to express the thought that everything that exists everywhere and anywhere are somehow equal within the guiding spirit that we call God.

The human being is invested with what some can consider as being called the Christ light which sets it above other things, but this only means that each human being should feel as though they were anointed by God as if a monarch, and as a monarch among monarchs and serving a supreme monarch should seek only the welfare of the others so anointed.

The human being thus feeling themselves to have each and every one a special role to play in the Great Spirit's scheme of things, should also deal with kindness and compassion to anything else, anywhere else.

God as the Great Spirit is all-pervading of life, both physical incarnate and spiritual incarnate and discarnate.

The human being is expected to repay the portion that is received of God's power by learning from the life experience and by so doing pass on the knowledge that they have gained to the next human being.

The human being has been given along with the portion of God's spirit, the extra responsibility as guardian of the world and has been given the gift of communication not just between human beings who exist in the here and now, but by sundry means to pass on information gathered from past generations for the benefit of future generations.

We hope that this communication between ourselves in the spirit realm and you who dwell presently on the earth plane has in some part at least answered your question.

Jan 8 2000

What is the greatest contribution Spiritualism has to make to the modern world?

In a world riddled with technological improvement, Spiritualism maintains the fiery torch and the wheel of spirituality and its progress.

Spiritualism is the saviour of the world, because it preaches unity and equality and unconditional love for all and, everything therein the world. There is no finer antidote to the ills of the world and to the fears of those who dwell within it at the present time than the tenets of a spiritual lifestyle as laid down by Spiritualism.

There is a need for Spiritualists to take their message out as though missionaries of old, but without the murder and mayhem that has previously been the missionary benchmark - or trademark.

We do not say convert or die, because we know that there is no physical death in the ordinary sense of the word, but spiritual deprivation is a terrible thing.

Some argue that the term Spiritualism is not appropriate, but there has to be some appellation to which people may refer, wherein lies a meaning that is comprehensible to them.

Spiritualism has begat Spiritualists, and it is the Spiritualist who is enjoined to take their belief out into the mainstream of human, consciousness and change the world for the better, to imbue the machine age with the knowledge of spirit, and the knowledge that that spirit will never die. God bless you all.

"There is no finer antidote to the ills of the world and to the fears of those who dwell within it at the present time than the tenets of a spiritual lifestyle as laid down by Spiritualism..."

Jan 15 2000

When dealing with the orthodox is it better to be gentle or harsh?

It is not suitable for those who would enlighten others to act in a domineering or authoritarian way, as truly spiritual people through all the ages have attempted to demonstrate, unfortunately mostly to their disadvantage on the material plane.

It is often said that the pen is mightier than the sword, and it is true that the spoken word, whilst a powerful ally to those who seek to spread in truth the realities of a spiritual lifestyle, it is as though the speech is written only on the wind, and may also often be, shall we say mistakenly, relayed orally, thus corrupting the original words, whereas if those words, the result of thought images, are committed to paper, they are thus preserved.

There is always the danger that such preservation also appertains to the delivery of untruths: this is the human condition with which we wrestle, and it must be said that whether spoken or written, the words which are corrupt or corruptible as well as the words which are truthful, both have their champions, and if only one side fights their corner in the eyes of the world, they become the victors.

Stronger words are needed for our fight. Orthodoxy will not fall of its own volition, but we caution those who would struggle against orthodoxy not to become as their avowed enemies are. There is more than ever there was, now a veritable spiritual army working for the enlightenment of the world. Count yourselves fortunate to be counted in their number, and by example we will win this war.

The shedding of blood is to be abhorred, but human nature being what it is, orthodoxy will be fuelled still for some time yet to come by this priceless earthly commodity.

Those in the spirit realms will continue to do what they can to guide and help you all towards the better times which will eventually come.

Keep on keeping on, and may the Great Spirit watch over you all.

Jan 22 2000

What will be the fate of war criminals in your world?

There is much work for them to be done on their own behalf of their souls. They are shown and experience without self-protection that was worn by them, created by them in their earthly life, the sufferings and torments of those for whose earthly fates they were responsible.

Because like clings to like in the spirit realms, they at first perceive themselves to be amongst those that they would consider friends. They arrive in the same sorry and sad paltry conditions as they left behind surrounding themselves.

It is not too long before they realise that they are objects of sorrow to those for whom they were tormentors in the earthly life. As they come to the realisation of their dreadful position in the order and hierarchy of the spirit realms so their progress begins.

It is a truly dreadful situation in which they begin this journey into the light which may well take many aeons of earth time, but the glory of God the Great Spirit is everywhere even in such infernal regions as those who perpetrate wickedness upon the earth are.

There is always hope for redemption of even the most vile of human beings because we all belong to the great Creator and some must crawl as the slug at the feet of the Giver Of All Life And Love before they can embark on the process of betterment of their own spirit.

There is so much to be learned by all God's children for so we all are and so they all are, but those who have allowed themselves to be swayed by and into wickedness, must find that fact out for themselves, before light can begin to be shed on their darkness.

Amen.

Jan 29 2000

What can they tell us about crop formations? I have had all sorts of explanations but have seen none from spirit.

The aberrant designs in otherwise natural environments are created by many different methods. One such being the hand of the human.

As many will be aware there is not much that can be done which will hoodwink spectators anymore in this new age of scientific exploration and discovery.

Nevertheless, some artificially induced phenomena in wheat fields and other areas of crop growing have almost escaped detection. It has been mooted that the Great Spirit is the master of design and therefore mathematics, and you will know that some of those designs emplaced in those fields of growing things are of a mathematical precision that mirrors all else in your known universe and which exist without it.

These are created using the electromagnetic spectrum, light and radio frequencies, that exist within your gravitational field on this planet. In spirit, there is no gravity, but gravitational pull is utilised also in the creating of these symbols.

It is not by mistake that they mirror other objects flying around in your universe, and in the future some will indeed be found to reflect the formations of other worlds too far distant for you to even contemplate at this time.

This is a communication to you from what you term the Spirit World, and therefore we do not concern ourselves with the earthly concepts of alien beings, nor whether or not such so-called alien beings are responsible in any part for the crop circle formations as they are commonly called.

We wish you to grasp the statement that there are no strangers in heaven or earth, only friends that you have yet to make and or meet. It is good that some mystery still occupies the minds of humankind.

May the natural world and the growing of edible crops be of sustenance to you in many ways of mind body and spirit. We come and go in peace.

May you also come and go in peace.

Amen

Feb 5 2000

Does every human being have a spirit guide?

Yes. You see all who are born into the physical incarnation have a motivating spirit within the physical framework.

In the human being that portion of spirit from the Divine Source of all Creation is intrinsically linked to the higher planes of life. Therefore that spirit, so dubbed higher spirit within, can be the guide of the human being and body in which it temporarily resides.

In this way, it can be said that everyone has a spirit guide, even if it is their own true self and not a discarnate spirit of loftier condition from the realms of light.

Those who seek to live in the light, even while they are dwelling in the realms of earthly gloom, should first develop sufficient insight to allow themselves access to their own spirit, and knowledge of its true motivation, and then to move on in their spiritual development in order to make that precious link between their own spirit and that of another independent, higher, more highly evolved spirit that may be called a guide from the spirit world, the finer illuminated dimensions of life.

Remember in all this searching for the meaning of life, and enquiry into matters esoteric, to keep as we do have a sense of humour. This comment is not as absurd as some may think. Let the spirit guide.

God bless you, and all of us.

"Those who seek to live in the light, even while they are dwelling in the realms of earthly gloom, should first develop sufficient insight to allow themselves access to their own spirit..."

Feb 12 2000

Why does not the spirit world give us proof of reincarnation?

We who serve the Great Spirit have often said at times such as these in answer to such a question, that no good purpose would be served by offering what would be unsubstantiated evidence of such an occurrence.

While we are all spirit, when we are in a physical incarnation it would seem foolish to consider any other such physical incarnations, and manifestations of what is necessarily perceived as prior occupation of an incarnate physical body.

Incarnation of spirit is of the utmost importance to those so incarnated, and they should occupy themselves with learning all they can to further spiritual development within such physical framework as has been given to them for the time being.

There should not be too much looking back to that of which the spirit incarnated may have experienced prior to this incarnation, only to review in the physical sense the one they occupy in the here and now.

To look into the future with hope and trust in the Great Spirit and to strive to achieve a measure of elevation and the kind of knowledge which can only be gleaned from a life on the earth plane.

Others may never visit the earth plane as incarnate beings, but this has a purpose too, and as all other purposes, is known only to that which all call God, the Great Creator.

The problem with the physical environment is that all physical manifestations relate back to it, and therefore stories of past incarnations are provable on the physical level only up to a limited point.

There is always room for conjecture and theorising, and this is not the way of establishing solid proof. Mr Darwin's theories are still being debated in this way, as are those of others who wish to explore the physical dimensions of life.

We who are, like you, of spirit, but who unlike you, dwell in the other realms of finer frequency, wish you well in your own discussions and debates on this particular subject, which occupies so many at the present time.

We enjoin you to live in the present and trust in the future and look forward to when we all shall meet again.

Feb 19 2000

Why do we ask God to forgive us our sins: for if the law is broken does not the penalty follow?

There are many interpretations of what constitutes the law. There are therefore as many different versions of transgression and perceived sin accordingly.

There is much said and written of what is called natural law but sometimes that could be taken to mean the law of the jungle could it not. Nature itself from which the word natural results and derives is itself red in tooth and claw.

The cries of women in childbirth were deemed to be natural and therefore to fall within both natural law and that which was said to be divine law given by God in the Biblical sense.

Therefore, you see in that case it would follow that those who sought to alleviate and relieve that female aspect of suffering would be transgressing both the natural law and divine law.

We leave you to consider the ethical ramifications of that particular instance. Some belief systems have it that the human being is born out of and in sin and that this has to be expunged in ways that they prescribe to their followers.

For others the wearing of particular garments would be considered full of sin where to other peoples such a matter would not even be worth the slightest consideration. It is only common sense to know that if you light a fire and stay too near you will be burned.

If you know that an action is wrong and that it will harm another whether it be of the human race or other, then the consequence to the perpetrator is always made manifest, and will cause at the very least discomfort of the spirit and then of course it follows as night follows day, the physical self.

One of humankind's greatest teachers constantly reiterated that all should love one another. When this love abounds then there can be no sin.

Where there is a lack of love both within the soul of an individual for themselves, it is difficult for that person to extend love to others, and that which exists around them, and it is from these loveless persons from which much that is generally to be considered as sinful ways, emanate.

All who are possessed of the Great Spirit on earth should try their singular best to establish perfection on earth as it is in heaven.

Thy will be done.

We can of necessity but scratch the surface of this particular debate in answer to such a deeply important philosophical question.

Feb 26 2000

Is it of any use that Armistice Services should go on, year after year?

Armistice is another way of declaring a truce or a ceasefire of hostilities between warring factions. It is therefore fitting to celebrate the end of such evil doing.

It is in truth the celebration of mutual forgiveness, but the way in which the day that you ask about is conducted gives rise to many feelings that could be related to those of the embattled and is accompanied by much militarily inspired pomp and circumstance.

Mr Elgar himself is horrified at the misuse of his music so named in support of an entrenched xenophobia. This was not his intention as a musician. Music is played too at these Armistice ceremonials and it is considered by many musical talents that this is a misuse of their work.

There is nothing to be gained by marching up and down in displays of nationalistic fervour, rather the Armistice should be celebrated as a memorial to those who were forced into war by the evil stalking the human race at that time, and should proceed accordingly with quiet prayer and spiritual songs.

The human race needs to remind itself of the evils that are done because of sectarianism, factionalisation, greed and corruption and that to make spiritual progress is of paramount importance to its welfare as a whole and not in the pursuit of individual materialistic gratification.

We would opine that it is necessary to have such a remembrance, but we say that this should take place at the beginning of every day of every year not on just one.

Until there is no war on earth it is just as well to have one day as a reminder of the foolishness that has taken place before it.

May peace come to the world. Amen!

March 3 2000

Would you say that guides are always spiritually in advance of their mediums?

Those who are in spirit only must necessarily be viewed as being in a more spiritual circumstance than those who are existing at the present time on the earth plane in the physical body.

Being spiritual is not dependent either on the intellect, whether incarnate or discarnate. This is where most confusion arises, particularly with regard to animals who now reside in the etheric world of finer vibration and who can be said to be of spiritual quality but are not particularly well equipped to act as guides, so often used as another name for mentor in spirit.

A guide is by definition one who delivers guidance to another in one way or another although it is most often used more generally in Spiritualist parlance.

This blanket term gives rise to some pondering on the part of those both on the earth plane and in the world of spirit.

The guide or guides who attach themselves to intermediaries on the earth plane are always more spiritually advanced than those they seek to help, otherwise it would be a case of two or more individuals enduring the same struggle to move themselves forward on their pathway, which could make for some interesting travels, but in the main it should be taken that the spirituality of a discarnate entity or entities having mind to assist those left on the earth plane are in advance of them.

It has always been known that those who have the higher ground have an advantage over those who occupy the valleys or planes, holding an overview therefore.

We would like to mention humankind's best friend the dog will always seek to raise themselves high off the ground, and we could do worse than to emulate that compulsion in a spiritual manner.

So the quick answer would have been to say yes.

God bless you all, and may the peace of the Great Spirit enfold you and lift you up.

March 11 2000

To what would you attribute the sudden increase in drug-taking and addiction, especially among young people? Can we offer any tangible aid to them?

There is a vast chasm between spiritual desire and material acquisition which is responsible for feelings of inadequacy for those whose gaze is forever directed at the world immediately surrounding them.

The habit of drug-taking for other than medicinal purposes has always been used to allow an escape from the mundane and otherwise earth plane based tribulations of the human spirit.

The ingestion of drugs that induce feelings of euphoria and spurious wellbeing enable short term relief for spiritual short-sightedness.

However, there is a high price to pay for these temporarily rose-tinted spectacles.

The problem of the young is that they are not empowered by their elders but feel themselves to be over restricted by those with authority over them in the physical sense and therefore their only redress in this situation as they see it is to disguise their feelings of inadequacy to themselves, and sometimes as a result, to others.

The society in which we have to live on the earth plane is primarily materialistically orientated and as such has a great deal of responsibility for the sad situation of substance abuse among the older population as well as the young and unenfranchised groups.

Until there is a parity of opportunity and substance of comfort and material needs met, this sorry state of affairs will continue unabated.

Spiritual values must be propounded for the benefit of all and particularly for the upliftment of the spirit and spiritual aspects of the human condition before alleviation can be found.

We sit in judgement on the perpetrators of these conditions and not the victims. Spiritualism should take the lead in bringing enlightenment to those who not only live in darkness of the material world themselves, but who because of their actions compel others to also dwell in darkness of their making, and not only that but chastise them for attempting to break out of it.

Let there be light.

March 18 2000

Where is the spirit, or that part which serves after death, when a person is under an anaesthetic?

The spirit is within, the spirit is unchanging, the spirit never sleeps, therefore it cannot be anaesthetised.

There are many recorded descriptions by persons who have been in deep anaesthesia but who are able to recall that which has happened to them while in such a condition of the physical self.

The spirit is as we know that spark which is of God, and which is indivisible from everything else. The spirit never sleeps.

What are the spiritual aspects of heart transplant surgery?

It depends very much on the interpretation of spiritual. Some apply this as meaning of the spirit when they really mean the soul. Some take it to have some ethical meaning.

Notwithstanding the semantics of the case, taking a physical organ from a body which of necessity is basically still alive, must have some ethical argument attached to it.

Similarly, the use of organs from animal kind particularly that which is nearest the human being, of the porcine family, is to be abhorred. There is nothing spiritual about the blatant use of one creature by another for its sole benefit.

We who are not of the physical world may perhaps be thought of as somewhat arrogant in our eschewal of transplanting organs in order to prolong physical life, but we say this because we must tell you the spiritual truth, and not make apologies for other trains of thought which owe much to the earthly existence and physical conditions within that.

May your spirit be ever vital and your soul be ever in the sight of God.

Remember life is eternal.

March 25 2000

Are Genetically Modified Foods Safe for Humans?

They are as safe as any other comestibles. They are to be compared with the difference between bread which is white in colour and the bread which appears brown made from unadulterated flours generally named wholemeal.

Genetically modified food is interfered with by scientific process from seed to fruition, and thereafter as is quite usual now. This process however denies the spirit of the force of creation and could therefore by definition be deemed lifeless, as we know we literally are what we eat.

So if we were to ingest only such processed substances so our energies would dwindle accordingly. This does not just apply to the human race.

Where animals and birds have been fed with inappropriately, inadequately processed foodstuff, the consequences are only now becoming apparent to those who have had the responsibility of so feeding them.

There is sufficient land in the world to grow plenteous crops in a natural way that pays due regard to that creative life force and good spirit.

The motive as usual is greed and not a desire to forward the development of the world and its inhabitants. The debate will continue on the earth plane and argument will rage until the awful consequences are generally known.

There is a danger of rendering life sterile in every department and this we can only counsel against. It is the responsibility of every thinking being to work this one out for themselves, and to examine all scientific data appertaining thereto, and to bring their findings and knowledge to the notice and attention of their fellows.

Meanwhile, those who are aware must be sure to feed and water themselves and their animals and birds and fish only naturally produced goods. We must all pray for enlightenment to dawn before it is too late to redress the balance of life.

God bless and keep you safe from all harm.

April 1 2000

Should religious leaders who discover these spirit truths renounce their old orthodox outlook?

Most orthodox religious leaders are already very aware of contact with the other worldly regions and dimensions, but they are constrained by their historic trains of thought and learning, which some may call indoctrination.

There is no doubt in the mind of those so elevated within their own belief systems that Heaven or Nirvana exists, or that there are other planes lesser than they are.

There are many religious leaders throughout the world's major faiths, who regularly meditate as part of their own disciplining, and who as a result of their own attainment and desire for spirituality do receive communication from the realms of spirit; but as a person thinketh, so they attract those to themselves who are very much of like mind, and it must be averred that ascension to the spirit realms does not immediately confer vast wisdom on spiritual matters to the entrant.

That is why it is sometimes considered to be some sort of religious club to which many belong, and of course those who were in the forefront of such organisation are the last to relinquish their own viewpoints on matters appertaining to their own spirit and that of others, and that which is deemed to be the world of spirit rather than the world of baser matter.

The truth, however, must be served, if not during a cleric's lifetime of whatever orthodox stream they belong to, then eventually, even if it takes an eternity.

We will not speak here of control or power or mind games, for you are all sufficiently aware of those arguments, but we consider that where people in high places on the earth plane know the truth, it is their duty to their own conscience to admit the truth, but you live in a less than perfect world and this is just one awful aspect of it from where we sit.

May the Great Spirit guide you on your spiritual pathways and keep you safe.

April 8 2000

How would you interpret the words "The love of the Great Spirit" and "To love our neighbours as ourselves"?

Love which is of the Great Spirit and emanates towards the Great Spirit is the unselfish desire to give goodness, kindness, compassion, as a selfless act, on the part of the one so doing, and is to experience that, in the receiving of it.

Neighbour can be taken to mean anyone else, other than oneself. To have a care, and a caring, and a respect for any other, as much as you should be able through your soul's evolution, to give to yourself.

It is only the individual who loves themselves who can truly love another. The Great Spirit is indeed just that, a great expansive and ever-expanding consciousness, a limitless intelligence in which true love resides.

Love is a much-quoted and much-misrepresented word too often allied with greed, and jealousy, and envy, and of course it is known that there is a very thin line between love and hate in its usual expression as an emotion, and not of the spirit-based self.

When love is used in a base animal context it has nothing to do with the Great Spirit in as much as the spirit transcends the physical and material world.

Of course, where one's neighbours being other inhabitants of the earth plane are concerned, the giver, givers, of love to each other, unfortunately are most prone to being unable to escape the physical emotional constraints that their earthly lives put upon them.

The easiest way in which spiritual love is conveyed is to call it unconditional, and in such a way those who are interested may understand that this love, by its definition, is not tied to any physical manifestation.

The love of the Great Spirit is thus unconditional and love given to the Great Spirit is also, and the love enjoined to be given to one's neighbours as though they were oneself, should also be qualified with the special word unconditional.

We send our unconditional love to you all, and to the Great Spirit, and our neighbours of which you may count yourself one.

April 15 2000

In cases where the patient creates the circumstances continuously which create the illness, is it part of the plan that healing should be given again and again?

Yes. We do not sit in judgement on anyone else's circumstances, nor on the conditions with which they surround themselves. It is not always easy to be strong-minded about these things when one is embroiled in the usual difficulties of the earthly life.

Without going into detail and case histories, it has to be accepted that there are weaker brethren among the stronger. The weak are to be helped unconditionally and at all or at any cost.

This is the prerogative and benefit to those who are strong, whether that be in mind or body, or dare we mention it, spirit. Earthly circumstances are sometimes unbearable, but nevertheless cannot be changed, and healing can assuage the pain suffered as a result.

Healers may only call themselves those who give healing whenever and wherever it is requested of them.

Their spirit helpers are only too gratified to find what one might call a difficult case requiring their help. It may, through the process of healing be possible to strengthen the innermost resolve of the earthly sufferer, and thereby effect an improvement in their situation.

As children we all may see problems encountered by those living in dire poverty and squalor, in what are called, 'underdeveloped' countries, and with a child's view, wonder why those so afflicted don't just move to somewhere more benign, with a better climate, soil, and therefore living conditions.

As we mature so we understand that it is not that simple, similarly, with those who suffer in mind and body because they are in situations and environments which are not conducive to them, but in which they find themselves.

Healing must continue regardless of any outward considerations.

May the light of the Great Spirit shed its healing rays through and upon you all.

April 22 2000

At what point after conception does a spirit enter the body of a baby?

It is at the point of fertilisation. At that point there is a cataclysmic explosion and implosion between the world of physical matter and that of the spirit dimensions and frequency.

Whether the spirit therein ever completes that first stage of the physical journey without is a matter for Higher Authority, as one may call the Great Spirit.

There are many and various ways in which this process is interfered with and constraints placed upon that journey, but the truth is not always palatable to those who would deliberately thwart the progress of such spirit.

We do not sit in judgement, nor at this time can we deliberate further on the ramifications of those who, being in the spirit world, may choose, or be chosen, to perhaps only reside for a microcosm of earthly time in the physical world.

Sometimes it is but a small part of a whole spirit that enters into the physical life frame. It may also be that the spirit of the individual knows in advance that they are not to incarnate outside of the womb, but these instances are too lengthy to elaborate upon for the purposes of this particular communication.

Some of us have never been visitors to the physical world. May the Source of all Life give strength to you in your quest for the truth and may the Great Spirit help you to deal with the discomforts and suffering that the truth always seems to bring on the head of the enquirer.

Love is indeed the great deliverer. We will speak again on this subject at a future date.

May you be aware of your own spirit existence and that of all others as being sacred.

April 29 2000

Would it be true to say that only the people who see beauty in this world will be able to appreciate it in the next world?

What absolute nonsense. There are some who while they live on the earth plane have no opportunity to find either themselves, or their fellows, or their environment, beautiful.

Nevertheless, these are the people for whom the heavenly hosts congregate at their passing, to usher them into a world of beauty such as you or I would never have dreamed of, even though we thought we lived amongst beautiful things, and perhaps even beautiful people and animals.

There are earthly conditions of such dire ugliness that the concept of beauty itself is lost, and unexplainable, to those who experience such ugliness.

There are many reasons for this situation to prevail, some of which are not too difficult to envisage. It is hard to find beauty in a world which starves and torments you.

It is hard to find the beauty in oppressive situations, and yet there is beauty in abundance waiting for those so impoverished of beauty in the earthly condition on this other side of life, the beauty of food, music, sleep, full consciousness, knowledge, nature duplicated in all its glory, for those who were denied such.

This is not to encourage early passing, for this only points to the need for social business to be undertaken by those who understand and enjoy beauty in their earthly lives on behalf of those who suffer so much. Those who are of a mind in the world of spirit are there assisting in such tasks.

There are some who are able to see beauty even though living in utter degradation, but these are the gifted of spirit, who in the knowledge of their own spirit self are able to rise above the earthly condition.

All should strive by economic means as well as spiritual to bring beauty into the lives of all who dwell on the earth plane.

God bless you all.

May 6 2000

Is the spirit world planning a further revelation by sending another teacher like Jesus?

There have been many teachers throughout the history, both recorded and unrecorded, of humankind.

The world in which you live at the present time is very different from the world that existed a few minutes ago, never mind thousands of years back.

The teacher Mohammed said that to every age its book, meaning that as times change and the awareness thereby of the world's inhabitants, so it is required that new teaching, such as that contained within a book, is necessary to be propounded and brought forth.

The teacher is only as good as the knowledge that she or he can draw upon and thereafter impart, and this to the satisfaction of the recipient of such. Not only have there been a multitude of good teachers bringing revelation from the world of spirit and those who sit closer to God, but there are nowadays such good teachers who make their presence felt, as there will be in all the time to come.

It is a circular race, with the baton of knowledge being passed on at every stage of development of the human race and its intellectual understandings, and one that has no end and no individual winner, but the whole of the human race will triumph, as the desire to transcend earthly limitations burns ever brighter in the human psyche.

What distinguishes the great teachers is purity of heart and inner communication with the highest spirit available to them, according to what is in their own innermost being.

This is what distinguishes individual teachers such as Jesus.

It is also the knowledge that they are as the lowest of any of their brethren, so deemed by social circumstance or religious diktat, and thus demonstrating the knowledge that all of Gods children are as one.

Amen.

May 13 2000

To what extent does destiny play its part in man's earthly life? Is predestination an outside force or your own choice? If you accept reincarnation, can you say why and what purpose it serves?

There is a certain quota of predestined occurrences in any one individual's life path. These are arrived at by the free choice of that individual interacting with their fellows who inhabit the same environment and those who fall outside of that involvement on a personal level.

By this we mean for instance government actions and actions taken by others also to whom the individual is unknown as a person. The question of reincarnation is a constantly recurring one.

While we do not speak of lessons learned on the earth plane, although this knowledge funds the greater pool in the realms of spirit, there are many aspects of any one soul belonging to an individual, and so it is possible to look philosophically rather than scientifically at any answer which is categorically in the affirmative or negative.

It is sometimes said that we who dwell in the realms of spirit actually return when we speak through our instruments and channels.

However, we will end as we began with a little joke, and say that we have a foot in both camps therefore.

"The question of reincarnation is a constantly recurring one..."

June 6 2000

Will you give your interpretation of the laws that regulate all life?

Law implies a set of rules and judgement, particularly should there be transgression, with an accompanying punishment.

Nevertheless, the laws governing life for the human race, rests upon that which is right and that which is wrong. It has been well written and often, that effect naturally follows on from the cause, and in a perfect earthly world this would be an appropriate effect.

There is however a grey area which often appears to seem to be favouring the wrongdoer, who often appears to be reaping a beneficial effect to themselves, rather than a bad one. When we speak of the soul of the human being, which is governed by spiritual law, that is a very different matter.

Those who seek to destroy others shall experience a canker that nibbles away at the substance of their soul material, having an effect on the physical self which has to be addressed sooner or later. If such a sufferer passes to the realms of spirit without mending themselves from within, as one might say, they will have to see to it thereafter.

The human being on the earthly plane is beset by many primeval urges, these are often quantified as seven deadly sins, of course there are many, many more.

It is difficult to ascend the path of righteousness, but the reward is great, for those who strive for the good in themselves and others, and for the world in which they live, will feel themselves to be bathed in the glory of the love of the Great Spirit.

The law is in each one of us, we know it is emplaced within us, the knowledge of what is good, and what is bad, what is right, and what is wrong, and as the law is in each one of us, so judgement and reward and punishment is vested in the individual.

All become aware eventually of the way in which they may err, and then set about repairing that. For is it not said that to err is human, but to forgive is divine. It is not correct to forgive without reparation, for without such, forgiveness does not exist.

All life is interlinked, is co-dependent, and unique at the same time. This includes the living both on the earth plane and in the other dimensions which includes the animal kingdom, flora and fauna.

There is an eternity through which all human beings may progress.

God Bless you all.

June 10 2000

Do you think that churches, chapels, and synagogues perform any useful purpose?

Yes. They provide a spiritual focus for the rather overly materialistic communities which they serve. The fact that the ceremonial, the ritual the dogma that underlies the potential for spirituality takes precedence in those places of worship to the knowledge of universal gifts of spirit, is however to be condemned.

It is good that individuals who may not otherwise consider cosmic questions such as the reason for their being on the earth plane in the first place, the purpose of their life, or indeed where that life is taking them and what will happen after the physical disintegrates, there have an opportunity to ponder. Although for the most part they will be told stuff which should not be acceptable or accepted by the spiritually intelligent.

There is no need for those who know the truth about spirit to feel compelled in any way to be or stay in any of those edifices, ostensibly built for the glory of God, but in reality does the Great Spirit and those in whom that Great Spirit dwells, a great disservice.

It is good for people of like minds to come together in a spiritual way to give thanks for the life they have received and the experiences within that life, whether those he considered by the individual to be good or bad.

It is fitting for those with knowledge of their own spirit and who have an acknowledgement of that sameness and oneness of spirit in others, to invoke healing vibrations which can only help them all and the world and the universe in which they dwell. In this way also of communion with their fellows on the earth plane to experience communion with their fellows in the world of spirit, by such congregation.

Once the spirit of the individual becomes known to the consciousness of that person, and the inner knowing becomes the progenitor of the understanding that spirit is all around and interlinked with that of the individual, so truly small buildings, microcosmic enclosed spaces, in the grander order of things, only become prisons, keeping that little independent life force and hall of energy and light that is the human being motivated by spirit.

Dwelling on the earth plane, walling the wonders of the natural universe away from them: but where love is that still must be the prime consideration wherever it may be found.

June 17 2000

Why are people left on earth unable to do anything for themselves, for example after a car accident? Why cannot euthanasia be put into practice?

Euthanasia is murder. Murder is the stealing away of the remaining earthly life of the individual. There is no justification for killing someone else.

There is a case for the administration where it is available, of medicines and unguents for the relief of pain where there is such. Spiritualist healers know much about the relief of painful symptoms even if there is a problem which means that the cause of the pain cannot be helped.

Human beings are born with a certain amount of free will and a great deal of personal responsibility, both toward themselves and others around them. The individual must choose right from wrong and know the difference.

If what may be called the left-hand path is chosen, then the individual so deciding will have to make reparation.

The physical body is only the vehicle of the spirit and, while the spirit is nourished and supported until such time as the physical body ceases to operate, so the spirit within must be respected above all earthly considerations.

The human spirit is knowing and wise and the physical material by which it is housed has a bearing on the sensibilities of that spirit, but it is of secondary importance.

If it is not much use, that is to be borne by the individual and sustained in whatever capacity it still has by other human beings. We are speaking on the day of the birth of one human being who, along with many others, was the victim of what some called justifiable euthanasia.

We point this out as justification should it be required for our argument against it. May the light and love of the Great Spirit forever shine upon you, each one of you, and you should live out your earthly life according to the Great Plan and none shall take it from you.

Amen!

June 24 2000

If you were asked to broadcast on the truth of Spiritualism, what would you say'?

First of all Spiritualism is a way of life. A philosophy and a science wherein all may behold the truth. Truth is an absolute. It is not an item which lends itself to being swayed or otherwise contorted by those who would seek to further their own ends by so doing.

Spiritualism is hope, is faith and is charity, in equal measures for all those who come to the understanding of that truth which stands so firmly embedded within it.

Spiritualism is the result of new understandings brought to bear on old misconceptions, the fact that all survive physical death, that the spirit within each and everyone continues in a conscious existence not reliant on any outside circumstantial factor, that used to be said, it may or may not lead to, it was indeed a giant step forward for humankind.

Spiritualism is the coming world religion. It is religion that makes perfect sense to the rational and reasoning human being. There is no pomp and ceremony that should attach itself in any way shape or form to the spiritual practice of the Spiritualist life and its acceptance of Spiritualism.

Spiritualism maintains and proves that all are equal, and that love without passion is the vibration within which we all operate, even those who struggle against it must be touched by the web of eternal light that gives them life itself. It is possible to identify the Spiritualist thread throughout recorded history, manifesting in those who would bring the glories of the eternal realms of light here on your earth plane, our earth plane, in attempts to elevate the lives of those living at that time around them.

The good that is Spiritualism will succeed, and peace and love will come to the earth in good time. All will be well. All is well. Prayers are constantly answered.

The good and positive thoughts offered up and out by those who understand Spiritualism, are heard, and Spiritualists know that they are heard, even amongst the angels who have the ear of the Great Source of all that ever was, that is and ever will be. So be it.

July 1 2000

Does guidance come from a general or particular source?

Guidance can come from both general and a particular source of information. The general source could be said to be that which is given after much discussion, debate, and argument in the classic sense of that word, by quite large cantonations of wise entities in the world of spirit.

There is of course a vast endless reservoir of consciousness wherein lies all the wisdom and knowledge and experience that has ever been and that will ever be, and sometimes it is possible for a particular soul to tap into that supply.

There are individual spirit entities who are able to draw upon their own store of such knowledge, which enables them to give such deep and meaningful information to any enquirer. Knowledge is for all to enjoy.

Wisdom comes in a different way. It is good to spread knowledge and with it we hope wisdom should also manifest itself. We all have our favourite avenues through which to acquire information.

This way is but one of many, and we are glad to be of service in the search for such. Wisdom will come as it surely must to all who seek that crown.

"There is of course a vast endless reservoir of consciousness wherein lies all the wisdom and knowledge and experience that has ever been and that will ever be, and sometimes it is possible for a particular soul to tap into that supply..."

July 8 2000

Is the Great Spirit within a separate entity, capable of reasoning, thinking and acting independently of the conscious self?

If you are suggesting that God the unknowable is a parody of any one individual here present or gone before from the earth plane the answer you know is flatly no.

The Creator of all things in both heaven and earthly spheres cannot be indicated in Biblical terminology. God is neither man nor woman nor fish, fowl, animal, vegetable or mineral, but to put it simply, and this is where the confusion enters the argument, all of these categorisations are indeed in a small part of the substance of God.

God the Great Spirit is omniscient and omnipresent, both the progenitor of everything and the things itself. There is a multitude of sparkling fragmentation like the twinkling stars and planets of the very universe itself which you can imagine as God thinking.

God the Great Spirit is everything. We who have a thoughtful awareness of that Great Spirit are responsible for all that takes place in the name of God, and for that which should have nothing to do with it.

The evil that dogs humankind is that part of the human psyche which the individual is required to vanquish. Indeed, it is the only victory which is worth anything in the name of God.

God is the source of our communication, as of every ability, availability for participation, in the life and life eternal, and for this we bless the Creator. Amen.

"We who have a thoughtful awareness of that Great Spirit are responsible for all that takes place in the name of God..."

July 15 2000

Why does not the spirit world interfere when it sees so many appalling atrocities committed on animals?

There is no way in which those who inhabit the realms of light may interfere in the doings of the human race except through the means of touching the spirit which the human being calls the heart, meaning the emotional response to love.

The human being is born with the freedom to choose right from wrong, and for this purpose was given also what is called a conscience through which their consciousness may operate.

The basic animal instinct of the carnivore is to kill for food. There are animals who toy with their intended prey after those have been caught, in order that special substances be released into that subject animal's system which thereafter renders the meat more to the predator's liking.

This is an unpleasant fact, and which may relate unfortunately to that animal called the human being at its most basic level. These instincts are born of the physical material that clothes the spirit which does not have such leanings, although that spirit can be tainted by base desires.

These predatory instincts of the body are necessary in order to procreate, and in this matter too is sometimes at odds with the spirit of love.

The eternal dilemma for the human race is to rise above the carnal physical state wherein the finer spirit finds itself, and to distance itself from wanting to inflict pain and suffering on others, both of its own species and that of what it may collectively deem to be the lower orders.

All life is born with the right to exist in harmony with its world, and while the animal kingdom is not invested with the reasoning and learning powers and faculties of the human being, is worthy of respect because above all, unlike human beings, other species tend not to make war between themselves and kill each other just for fun.

Eventually those who are spirit incarnate will be as loving and wise as spirit discarnate in the realms of light, and so an end will come to the torment suffered by the animal kingdom, it is the will of the Great Spirit that this should be so.

May the light and love of the Great Spirit pervade your life and imbue your soul with love for all God's creatures.

July 22 2000

is a medium's health affected by trance mediumship?

It should be affected for the better. Before the medium becomes receptive to earthly enquiries he or she should have made personal contact with those in the spirit world with whom they work, and at this point in the proceedings those who wish the medium well in every respect could advise as to their general well-being.

You may be interested to know that before you asked that question, of which we were aware in advance, we were speaking to our medium, our instrument, about her health situation and were explaining a previous message given to her by another medium recently.

A medium who sits for their development as what is called a trance instrument of spirit must understand that they do have to take particular care of themselves in both the physical and mental condition.

All who are of the physical are virtually wearing out their physicalness from the moment they arrive in the physical world, and by allotting some of that physical energy to the world of spirit from whence they came, and towards which they are inexorably going, they will run the risk of infinitesimally accelerating that process.

Therefore it is wise to be abstemious of lifestyle in order to preserve the physical body.

As for the act of trance mediumship itself, this must be undertaken in appropriate surroundings, wearing appropriate clothing and without undue strain being put upon the physical body of the medium.

This naturally includes not fuelling the body for an hour or two at least beforehand. Trance mediumship is related to physicality and should be viewed as an athletic pursuit, and not just of the mind.

We wish all who offer themselves in this way our wish for their good health in every way and offer the blessings of the Great Spirit to all.

"Therefore it is wise to be abstemious of lifestyle in order to preserve the physical body..."

July 29 2000

Can you explain something of the plan that is behind spirit communications?

There is only one plan and that is to benefit earthkind. Ever since the beginning there has been a problem with the negativities required by physical earthly laws.

Where there is positive there has to be negative, or otherwise everything of the world in which you live would literally fall apart, but figuratively speaking, negativity of the intellectual kind could well be done without.

However, it is a fact both literal and in the realms wherein fancy dwells. This necessity has been causing much disruption and discontent and difficulty since the whole sequence of events began.

In simple terms, the magnet nor that which is electrical could function without the two disparate poles of negative and positive being present.

This physical fact has given rise to those thoughts and even imaginings by human beings about the nature of their own immaterial spirit which drives them, starting with black and white, dark and light, bad and good, wrong and right.

The first allusions are to the material and the last to the spiritual and one should not relate to the other condition and yet it seems manipulated by some so to do.

Our plan is to constantly demonstrate that there does not have to be a negative aspect within the spiritual attainment and aspiration, that the negative needs to be abhorred and vanquished, so that the spirit of the earth may live in a more positive, harmonious atmosphere now and forever.

"Our plan is to constantly demonstrate that there does not have to be a negative aspect within the spiritual attainment and aspiration..."

August 5 2000

Do you think laughter at seances is beneficial to results?

Laughter is always beneficial provided that it is not ever at someone else's expense. Seance is a word that moves in and out of fashion, and just now we note that it is becoming fashionable again.

However, we do not expect to see a resurgence of dinner wear at such events. There is much to be said for good humour in any situation, but particularly it helps to raise the spirits in more ways than one.

We must add that nervous laughter is not particularly conducive to the séance room as in conditions of black-out when it does sometimes occur. While we understand very well the requirement for sitting in thick darkness for the manifestation of some physical phenomena to manifest itself from our world of spirit, and we might say, material, there are other occasions where it is now possible to work with operators on the spirit side of life and instruments on the earthly side without worrying about the light frequencies therein.

We ourselves while on the earth plane would have found it extraordinary to have sat at a séance in the light, but now we communicate in such a way that the earthly light frequencies do not impinge upon our communication.

Often comical songs would be sung to raise the vibrations for a seance taking place in dark conditions. and these would generate much laughter and indeed happiness.

It is good to be happy in the presence of our loved ones in spirit, and even in the presence of angels and the Great Spirit itself.

May you always, all of you, find loving laughter within your soul.

"There is much to be said for good humour in any situation, but particularly it helps to raise the spirits in more ways than one..."

August 12 2000

How Does an Avowed Materialist Fare When He or She Passes Over?

Well, depending on how they have lived their lives, they could fare very well indeed. It depends very much on what is meant by materialist.

If we speak of one who worships mammon and is consumed in their life by selfishness and greed, which is the desire to feather one's own nest at all cost no matter to whom this cost applies, they will find themselves in a very sorry state.

As they have lived their lives in spiritual darkness, there will be no change on the immediate transition to the spirit realms. They will still be living in a fog until such time as kindly helpers and teachers will show them the way forward, the pathway that they should have taken whilst still in their material and materialistic form.

There is of course another kind of idealistic materialism which only seeks to better the material lot of their earthly brethren and sorority. These are they who, although rejecting the religious aspects of life, nonetheless have a spirituality about them which may transcend that of the next overly religious, in the orthodox sense, person.

There is a spiritual case to be put for that kind of materialist and we would hope that this sort of materialism could find natural expression within a Spiritualist context. It was said in ancient days that man cannot live by bread alone, but it is also called the staff of life and is necessary to feed the body that clothes the soul for the earthly timespan.

There must be ethical ways applied to the provision of this bread as well as clear water. This ethical application is totally linked to all that is best in the world of spirit. So the material world and materialism may serve the highest in spiritual endeavour.

Such a materialist would find themselves welcomed by good souls when they take their transition and for their goodly intentions truly find themselves in heavenly halls and pastures green and pleasant, such as, for all their earthly interest in bettering that material world, they may well never have experienced while they were on earth. Schweitzer and Russell and Mother Teresa are that kind of materialist of which we speak, among so many other good people.

> "The Great Spirit was able to fragment its consciousness, at least the lower elements of it, and create the living creatures..."

August 19 2000

What is your view as to the reason for the creation of a universe?

The Great Spirit, the Infinite Intelligence, created a universe which would have had an inbuilt loneliness within it, therefore the Great Spirit was able to fragment its consciousness, at least the lower elements of it, and create the living creatures for the company it would afford.

In so doing and in choosing to give those individual consciousnesses free will and freedom of choice, so those individual personalities begin to make their way home to the Great Spirit itself over an eternity.

This passage home is mirrored in every living thing, and the one most obvious might be that of the marine life which constantly pursues the place not of its physical birth but of its creation. In physical terms, its conception.

We of the higher orders of life as a human race understand that all things being equal, thought which is father to the deed must come first, just as it did in the beginning; so it is and ever will be.

Amen.

"It is possible for someone to be attuned to the world of spirit from which they have come in a naturally occurring way, should their physical self or physical environment not preclude it..."

August 26 2000

Mediums, must they be born or can they be trained?

Well, of course, the answer to that question is both. All are born with a psychic ability; it is the sixth sense with which we are invested, as are other living things. It is something which is said by physiologists to be linked to the endocrine system.

However, the psychic manifestation of the physical being is indeed linked to the body etheric, and through that to the spirit within, and through that to the spirit environment without, and through that to individual spirit, and through that to the Great Spirit.

It is possible for someone to be attuned to the world of spirit from which they have come in a naturally occurring way, should their physical self or physical environment not preclude it, but usually this ability to receive input from the world of spirit needs to be rediscovered by the ordinary person living an ordinary kind of life.

This faculty of mediumship can be developed in most people who have in the first place a desire so to do, because it is not an easy path; it requires dedication and often seif-denial, which is never easy.

It is not necessary to either live or have lived the life of a so-called saint in order to be able to become an intermediary between heaven and earth, but it is good that those who embark on such a course should endeavour to improve their innermost selves to become more selfless and to wish for the good oi others.

There are many good teachers now, although some lifestyles are not what we would have chosen; nevertheless, if the teaching is good and produces good and spiritually motivated mediums, then the shortcomings of the teachers may be forgiven.

We wish you all a more fulfilling and spiritual life, and happiness in the spiritual sense of the word.

Never forget that to attain the highest you must set your sights as high as possible, like attracts like.

God bless you all.

"It is not necessary to either live or have lived the life of a so-called saint in order to be able to become an intermediary between heaven and earth..."

September 2 2000

What is the greatest aid in spiritual progress, love or knowledge?

The key word here is 'spiritual', and it follows, as sure as night follows day, that spiritual follows love. Love is the most important emotion and feeling that exists, and there is no spiritual progression without it. Knowledge, on the other hand, is not everything in itself, for knowledge may be put to very unspiritual purpose or use.

When we speak of love, we do not refer to the rather downgraded versions of that which seems to permeate earthly situations at the present time, such as that which is associated with carnal desire - which may be an expression of a love, as it is sometimes described - but we speak of the highest selfless and unselfish desire to bring comfort and feelings of wellbeing and worth to others.

Knowledge can produce progress and that progress produces more knowledge, but one has to be discerning in its application. If love is present where there is knowledge, then spiritual progress should be attained thereafter.

We love knowledge and aspire to spiritual progress.

May God bless you all in your desire for spiritual knowledge with love.

"When we speak of love, we do not refer to the rather downgraded versions of that which seems to permeate earthly situations at the present time..."

September 9 2000

What happens when you become the channel as a healer?

In much as the same way that is demonstrated by any medium for communication from spirit, the healer who is used as an instrument by those in spirit is also required to have similar awareness of spirit.

The spirit of course of themselves, their own spirit self, that of the person who requires healing ministry, and those in spirit with whom the other two are to make connection with.

The development and the unfolding of gifts of the spirit should be the same, no matter what discipline the medium undertakes to participate in. Healing sometimes takes other qualities other than those which are required for clairvoyance, clairaudience clairsentience etcetera, may we suggest patience as a paramount attribute.

Healing may take a considerable amount of earthly time in every way, and it may be that a recipient of healing may not want to become fully healed for many and diverse reasons that may appertain to their earthly characteristics and personality.

Some who come to a medium for healing may in truth have nothing whatsoever the matter with them except for a loneliness of the soul, at one end of the heating spectrum, and at the other end we have those who approach the healer in agony at the end of their earthly life span; but at either end, and all shades of suffering between both mental and physical, the gifts of the spirit are bestowed in order to alleviate and spread love and knowledge of life as it is lived by spirit, as we all are whether in the physical sense or etheric vibrations.

Healing is the quiet mediumship, but it touches the spirit and soul of all who are involved in the process. There is much still to be done.

God bless you all.

"We love knowledge and aspire to spiritual progress…"

September 16 2000

Does spirit need contact with the world of matter in order to gain conscious individuality?

No. The material world is precisely just that. It has no spirit until that which is from the spirit dimensions, as ordered by the Great Spirit, enters into it. It is spirit that animates matter, not the other way round; that would be a reversal of the spiritual law which is on a par with natural law.

Individual spirit personality enters matter in animate creatures at what is called conception. It occurs in much the same way as the fertilisation process requires the meeting and blending together of two, so spirit, as consciousness, meets and blends with that matter of physical body that is being created.

It is not the other way round. Similarly, at the demise of that animated physical body the spirit which entered at its beginning moves on into the finer spiritual dimension, where as a conscious individual personality it will continue to develop without necessity of recourse to matter in the material sense.

It has been mooted that other things apart from human beings only survive as a projected memory of any particular human being, and we take this opportunity to refute that hypothesis.

The conjecture is not worthy of its proposer. All life is eternal where there is any self-awareness.

The microbe does not possess that. We hope that our answer is found to be acceptable in the light of reason.

May the Great Spirit of all things be with you.

"Some who come to a medium for healing may in truth have nothing whatsoever the matter with them except for a loneliness of the soul..."

September 26 2000

How would you explain the Great Spirit to children?

The medium was pondering this question before it was asked by yourself, so we are able through the medium to answer both she and you.

The Great Spirit is that which created all things, everything we know about, everything of which we are aware in the very beginning before everybody was born, and even before the planet on which we live and planets which surround us in the sky.

The Great Spirit is called God in general by other names depending on what religion or background one grows up in, and by some groups of people is not even given a name in case that would be disrespectful of that almighty power which we call the Great Spirit for want of worrying about grander names.

It suits the purpose very well we think. The Great Spirit is all around us and within us. It is the impetus which means the driving force which makes us want to do things for all those other people and things, such as our planet, in a good and positive way.

Some groups of good people from various backgrounds make dollies to represent their idea of what the Great Spirit must look like and of course we must remember for those who are not able to see such objects it is then possible for them to feel the shape by touch.

We say it matters not how people of the world choose to make the Great Spirit appear to themselves because the reason which makes them desire to know what the Great Spirit is in simple human terms, is a good one.

You know that a physical shape or form or body can never imitate the boundlessness of the Great Spirit, and it is that knowledge that dwells within your heart when you know the truth that is all you need to sustain you in this life and then in the world of spirit afterwards.

May the Great Spirit bless you, heal you and keep you safe. May you the children take the message forward. Amen.

"The Great Spirit is all around us and within us. It is the impetus which means the driving force which makes us want to do things for all those other people and things..."

October 4 2000

Would it be true to say that each reflection of the spirit has to work out its own progress, and the common benefit from the lessons learned by other reflections of the same spirit?

A very prettily put question. The concept of a reflection of spirit which we take to mean a reflected image of God, the Great Spirit, would deny substance to the individual spirit.

A reflection is only something mirrored. It has no real body itself. Each individual spirit is indeed a part of the whole picture, but it has its own freedom of conscience to choose the right path.

A reflection can only mimic that of which it is a two-dimensional depiction. It is possible to be, without recourse to the learning to which you refer. There is the ecstatic state which some would call the condition of just being at one with the universe in which they reside and God.

This does not require prior study, only a wish for inner betterment of the self.

This is not to say that acquiring knowledge is a bad thing, for this is how material progress is made, but spiritual progress is so often achieved by clearing self-centred thoughts from the mind and entering the condition of just being. We would suggest that an exercise of that nature undertaken every now and again at chosen intervals in any physical individual's life, will be of benefit to their progress and that of others around them as a consequence.

May you bathe in the reflected light that emanates from the Source of All Creation. So be it.

Amen.

"May you bathe in the reflected light that emanates from the Source of All Creation..."

October 11 2000

Do Our Spirit Friends Hear Us at All Times when We Mentally Speak to Them?

There are many levels and layers of the section on both sides of what has been called the Great Divide, just as someone may mishear when spoken to on the earth plane, particularly small children, so those in the world of spirit may not be able to hear at all times.

This is where the great answering service comes into its own, naturally presided over by the Most High, the sphere where all is known and therefore heard. These thoughts that are sent, such as supplications that are made, are, if you like, recorded and can be played back to the hoped-for recipient who resides in the world of spirit.

That is why sometimes it may seem that your thoughts are not immediately acted upon, but again earthly urgencies are not always those of the spirit realm.

The short answer would have been yes, but it was thought appropriate to express some of the difficulties that accompany trans-dimensional communication.

May God speed all your thoughts with love.

"There is the ecstatic state which some would call the condition of just being at one with the universe in which they reside and God..."

October 18 2000

Are we making serious mistakes in our approach to the world in general? If we are, could you enlighten us on these mistakes?

It is a fact of life on earth that mistakes are inevitable. It is by mistakes that we learn. We learn about ourselves, our environment and about other people and the creatures among whom we live on this planet.

There are however guidelines and guidance which is given as a result of knowledge gained by those who have gone before you and made mistakes, but it is said that you may not learn necessarily by reference to other people's experience of making mistakes.

The only way a human being can avoid making mistakes is possibly to be kept coddled against the world at large from its birth, even then by the laws of nature mistakes would have to be made.

The fire would have to be touched, the ice explored, the wrong food consumed and the wrong person annoyed. This is referring to the individual mistake maker, but it lends itself to the greater picture.

En masse many mistakes have been made, but the beauty is in rectifying them and by so doing making progress and that will ultimately benefit all.

The problem is that when you look back over the history of the human race, the same mistakes are made over and over again, and the price has to be paid over and over again.

Nevertheless, progress will be made and we must all aspire to the foundation of heaven on earth, a time when all those mistakes will fade into history, and only the remedy will remain.

All will be well. Those who dwell in the spirit realms or heaven will continue to aid those who are of good intention and good-spirited.

There is much work still to be done and more mistakes to be made, but thereby lieth the achievement and progress of the soul.

"Those who dwell in the spirit realms or heaven will continue to aid those who are of good intention..."

October 28 2000

Would you say that guides are always spiritually in advance of their mediums?

This is always the case because the mediums, the interlocutors' dwell in the gross matter of the physical plane of life, and therefore are prone to all those material distractions which cause them to have to struggle with the achievement of any level of spirituality within those confines.

Guides and helpers who have attained the higher life in the world of spirit of finer vibration and density, are able to express within themselves, and to those and that which are around them, a true spirituality without hindrance.

This does not mean that mediums should not strive for a greater understanding of their spiritual needs and the spiritual desires of others as though a spirituality would be too difficult therefore to achieve in the material life, but they should continue with their spiritual development in order that they may blend for the better with their helpers and guides in the spirit realms.

There are many paths by which spirituality may be achieved and accumulated in the worldly life. There are many valid systems that produce people of great spirituality, but communication with those who reside in the world of spirit is of paramount importance to the pathway called Spiritualism.

Therefore, it behoves Spiritualist mediums to try to emulate the lifestyle of their guides and helpers as much as they possibly can.

All difficulties regarding this matter are understood only too well by those who serve the same cause in the realms of light. We work on together.

We love and labour still.

"There are many paths by which spirituality may be achieved and accumulated in the worldly life..."

November 4 2000

Why do the loved ones who have gone into the spirit world always know what the people left on the earth are thinking?

It is not for the next person to ever know what the next person to them is thinking at any given time. The fact that one resides in the world of spirit does not immediately confer upon one the right to invade the individual privacy of the spirit, that is of someone else.

It is possible to comprehend signals of language that are sent out from the earth plane to the spirit realms and as we understand, to send them back again. That is, after all, the basis of communication that has been established between the two worlds.

Thought is the progenitor of the deed, and actions which are carried out, and therefore, by those actions, the thoughts that underly them are recognised.

The Great Spirit knows all and through the instruments of that Great Spirit some of the thoughts of those on the earth plane are made apparent to those dwelling in the spirit realms. Everything is by the grace of the Great Spirit.

It would not do if individuals were constantly privy to the thoughts of others, whether on earth, or in heaven- It is wise to always strive to have good thoughts, however difficult that may be at times, because God is your constant confidante.

May you live your lives on earth and in the heavenly spheres in the light of good thought. If you send out your thoughts to those who love you in the spirit world, they will be heard.

Have no doubt about that. God bless you.

"Therefore, it behoves Spiritualist mediums to try to emulate the lifestyle of their guides and helpers as much as they possibly can..."

November 11 2000

To what extent does destiny play its part in man's Earthly life? Could you describe destiny? Is predestination an outside force or your own choice? If you accept reincarnation, can you say why and what purpose it serves?

There are many pathways mapped out for the earthly being to choose which one they may take but they are never fixed, and they often intertwine, thus making it a simple job to cross from one road to the other.

It is possible by this method to go to the side or forward but regretfully never back on oneself. Going back is merely an illusion and has no substance to it.

Progress is an in-built requirement for every human being. There are what might be termed staging posts, where certain events and experiences are to be found. A little like the childhood game of hide and seek, or hunt the thimble. Sometimes with momentous consequence for the finder.

There are some earthly pathways which serve better spiritual purpose than others. These are very often the rocky paths, the uncomfortable and downright hellish, but these are the paths of those who would aspire to the spiritual heights which such struggling best suits them for.

There are easier options, and these result in perhaps imparting a lesser understanding to those who take them. These pathways through life are endless, just as life itself, but there are opportunities of a different nature in the spirit dimensions alone.

Although each individual has by definition a single pathway, there are always companions on their routes. These may be of a physical constitution or of spirit only.

Always the thread of life is bound to the Universal Source, who we may refer to, to give added colour to your thoughts, as the Great Weaver. This will give you some idea of the complexity of every life.

The knotty problem of whether or not the spirit enters again into a different physical bodily earth life is one that has occupied the unravellers of the mysteries of life since time began.

We say again there have been such instances; that we do not care to embark on a debate, which will go on for much time to come, both on the earth plane and in the lower realms of the spirit dimension.

We wish you all a great peace at this time in your lives and in the world which you inhabit still.

November 18 2000

What Makes One Person a Better Healer Than Another?

There is no such thing as a better healer because if there were there would also have to be a category of a worse healer, and that as you can plainly work out for yourself would be a paradox in terms.

A healer is anyone who wishes to give comfort to another of God's creatures or even one who cares for that which grows or is part of the globe on which they live.

Those who have an awareness of helpers who wish to give healing themselves from the world of spirit to those who are still suffering in the physical world may be more effective in an obvious way to those who they wish to help and among those willing souls in the flesh, there is no differentiation.

The differences are perceived by the recipients of their ministrations and are subjective in their assessments.

It is a good thing to strive on an individual basis for betterment of what may be considered the healing ability because it makes for a clearer channel through which the healing energies may be transmitted. We speak here only of the spirit and not the physical self, or its proclivities.

All who wish to give healing are blessed by the Great Spirit and in giving healing. They themselves receive healing. There is no healing balm more effective than the love which pours from the Great Spirit. It is available to all.

Remember healing is treatment for dis-ease not necessarily a cure in the ordinary sense of the word.

We wish you all better.

"Progress is an in-built requirement for every human being. There are what might be termed staging posts where certain events and experiences are to be found..."

November 25 2000

Are group souls family groups, people in the same state of spiritual development, those with the same interests, or what else?

The group soul is often misunderstood. It is not a homogenous lump of spirit material made up of individual consciousness as though those individual personalities were in some way missing the rest of themselves.

The group soul is made up of conscious beings, individual of spirit who have meaningful and constant interaction with each other on the various levels in which those in spirit, as well as those who presently inhabit the physical, reside.

Within the group soul, there is scope for general advancement through debate, discussion, and the pooling of experience. There are group souls which are indeed familial in every respect. There are also members of soul groups who are not physically genetically related.

There are many different ways in which the group soul may express itself. Ultimately the group soul becomes one with the Great Spirit, the Universal Soul, and although self-identification may alter with the progress made through time, that unique spark which comes from the Divine remains individual and applies to the persona of that which carried it.

No need to fear, therefore, oblivion nor obliteration by any individual. For being a part of the group soul to which that individual belongs, so the other members of that group cherish and protect each one of their number within the love of the Over Soul, the Great Spirit, that which is called God, the Creator of all that is, from the beginning and forever.

We who are aware now as we have moved on in the spirit realms, are aware of each member of our group soul, as you will become aware, are pleased to shed a little light on such a complex subject.

God bless you all, and your groups.

December 2 2000

What is the limit to speed of travel by spirits?

There is no limit to the spirit world. There are no limits to the Divine Light, although it has been fashionable to consider God's presence as being a circle, that in itself would describe a limited capacity for what would happen without the circle.

The speed of thought is amazingly rapid and faster than physical light, but thought generated by the brain is constrained by the physical environment in which, and under which, it operates.

When that thought is transferred to the mind, which is of the spirit being, there are no such problems, you might call that transference within a microcosmic moment almost simultaneous in the transmission and its reception.

Speed as you know is also subjective and varies through the perception of the participant. It also varies objectively as has been demonstrated by the comparison of the timing registered by chronographic means, after flights in aeroplanes around the world, in the physical sense.

Were we to undertake a similar experiment in the etheric dimension, we would doubtless have some similarly interesting calculations to ponder? Time is experiential and its own arbiter.

It could be opined that everything that occurs is in the present for someone, somewhere.

The knowledge that everything that has happened in the past, as perceived by human beings, is happening now, is a great burden when it is considered, a weight of responsibility, and in existentialist terms the present, which is the sum total of time spent in the past, has to he made acceptably spiritual and good for all creation, in order for the future to be a better proposition.

We who lived on earth in your past, speak to you all now in your present. We will all move into the future together. May it be as bright and beautiful as humankind and all related creatures, and yes, your planet itself, deserves.

May the Great Spirit be known to have the time for you.

Life is timeless.

December 9 2000

To what would you attribute the sudden increase in drug-taking and addiction, especially among young people? Can we offer any tangible aid to them?

Human beings are all born with what is called an addictive personality because they need to be addicted to certain things in order to sustain their physical life.

You may say that they are addicted to feeding and drinking and it is an aberration of this need with which the physical body is programmed that can so easily prompt the human being into constantly craving for that which does not do them any good at all.

It is also a fact that the spiritual self that in the young may find itself struggling against the physical constraints of its physical environment both of its body and the place wherein it lives that causes it to chase after an artificially induced vision of what it might feel like to be more of spirit and less of the physical self.

The way of life which is fully cognizant of the spirit within and the spirit without can give much comfort to those who rail against their misfortune to be bounded by physicality. The knowledge that we are all one that love is everything and material conditions of no real importance can prevent young human beings from a path that may lead them into a spiritual quagmire.

One that is very hard to drag oneself away from. Although of course it has been done. Meditation without the aid of substance abuse would be of enormous benefit to those so afflicted with cravings. Spiritualists could set up such places to which young people of all kinds and conditions without criticism or judgement could attend to receive spiritual upliftment.

The unfoldment of their own potential through mediums who would give guided spiritual journeys just as they might in any other circle. Spiritualists have a duty of responsibility to rescue those, their brothers and sisters on the earth plane, who are in such need.

There should be a concerted effort made before things get much worse. We do not wish to appear as Jeremiah, but neither do we feel that behaving like ostriches serves any good purpose in this matter.

May you all feel that you have everything that is necessary to your life and progress, and in the comfort of spirit and the Great Spirit never crave for more.

Amen.

December 16 2000

Fundamental to the Christian doctrine of the Atonement is the conviction that it is essentially the work of God, who, in Christ, reconciles mankind to Himself. Do you agree?

No. The only atonement or at one meant that can be made is within the spirit of oneness.

There is no way in which the purpose of earthly life can be served by the use of a scapegoat which is firmly lodged in the beginnings of humanity's striving for civilisation in the same times wherein the myth of the crucifixion of the Great Spirit made one man has its origin.

There is no one being of any kind that can absolve the guilty from their actions.

There may be forgiveness from the sinned against to the sinner, but the perpetrator of any transgression must find the way to make good their wrongdoing for themselves and ensure as much as anybody can on the earth plane that compensation and retribution be paid.

God gave the human being a consciousness an innate knowledge of basic ethics. The difference between right and wrong. It is this conscience that is to deal with atonement and nought else.

It is the personal responsibility of every individual to remedy their shortcomings and thus to progress their own spiritual pathway through this life and the next.

There is no easy route to salvation. Amen.

> *"God gave the human being a consciousness an innate knowledge of basic ethics. The difference between right and wrong..."*

December 23 2000

What is the use of man's earthly experience bearing in mind it is so limited in comparison with eternity?

The human being is a physical manifestation of the spirit of God, the Great Spirit, and therefore the human spirit is required to participate in a physical life form in order to fulfil that particular aspect of its spirit.

Should there be no manifestation in the physical, there would be a lack of understanding that is necessary to being able to call oneself human.

There are some presently in the world of spirit who have never yet incarnated into the flesh, but there will come a time even for those most spiritually highly evolved when they will be required to visit the earth plane with its physical constraints.

The physical experience is as you know very rarely pleasant, even in the midst of a physical enjoyment there is often a spiritual sadness. Marrying the physical with the spiritual is the main reason for the human earthly existence.

It is possible however for the spirit incarnate to rise above the physical plane when it is found to be a necessity, perhaps when the body needs some respite, and this is often a discipline that is practised tor the good of the practitioner and others who may benefit, such as through mediumship.

Life itself hangs on an eternal thread, the silver cord that binds everyone to the source of all life. and part of that line is designated for some earthly life experience.

There is no time in eternity only experience, and this can seem sometimes short and sometimes long, depending on what is being experienced at the time. At this time of the earthly year there is many an experience to enjoy or to endure. It is no accident that this time of year lends itself to a general experience of desire to touch spirit.

This is when the universal human being feels that they want to reach out into eternity to become yet again once more purely of the spirit; to connect once more with that which is all-pervading and good.

This is a time when the human being incarnate reaches out to the discarnate. both in themselves and in others. and may experience the feeling of being eternal and at one with the Great Spirit.

May the light of the Great Spirit of all the universes be with you all at what may seem a less than bright time. but to know that in the end on the earth plane there will be peace love and goodwill amongst all God's creatures. It has been said before that the lion will lie down with the lamb.

So be it. Amen!

January 6 2001

Was Jesus Christ "God the Son" as the Church says or was he an ordinary man with great mediumistic powers?

The man of whom you speak was neither of those things and yet both. He, like every other human being of the male gender, can be described as God the Son, God who is made the Son, as can every female be described as God the Daughter, the embodiment of God the Great Spirit in Woman.

There was not however very much of the ordinary about the man known now as Jesus. There are many born to the earthly life with mediumistic abilities, but very few attain the level of spirituality and goodness that can be attributed to the one called Jesus.

In other respects though you could say that in the physical sense he was an ordinary man. Great pains have been taken to point out his humble origins and artisan skills, but we also hear of his learned outpourings and biblical scholarship, both in ancient texts, and like this, in more modern revelations.

The pity is the division that has been caused for the human race which has cited the various strands of thought about this great man's work for the last many, many hundreds of years.

There is no doubt that sincere followers of this man's teachings and emulators of his lifestyle are to be commended. Imagine if you will his thoughts, as he perceives now from the realms of light. As one who sits at God's right hand, when he views the sadness and misery that is caused by such division between God's creatures on the earth plane.

The great hope for the future for one such as he is that the knowledge of what is truly right and good shall not only be known throughout the world but will be put into practice before too long.

Hold fast to that which is right, hold fast to that which is good, and all will be well.

May the Great Spirit bless all your effort in this direction. Amen!

"The great hope for the future for one such as he is that the knowledge of what is truly right and good shall not only be known throughout the world but will be put into practice..."

January 13 2001

Where healers are unable to see the aura, in what way can they work to know they have got the right attunement?

Healing that is accomplished with the assistance of guides and helpers in the spirit realms has no need to rely on physical signals such as the aura.

There are many who are adept at spiritual healing as it is most commonly called who would not know an aura if they saw one.

Those who work with healers from the spirit only side of life work on the spiritual substance of the being needing the healing, and thus affect an easement of the earthly conditions affecting the physical body of the recipient of their ministrations.

The spiritual self is a matrix of light which is mimicked by the aura which lies as a physical energy field a little way around the physical structure.

When the physical structure is no more. this aura is not there either, but a spiritual material which is like a rainbow bubble in appearance seething with colour and vibrating on a wonderfully fast frequency is the vehicle for the spirit which is forever in being, an eternal substance.

It is this etheric body of light which receives the healing, and from which benefits the physical which it interpenetrates.

It is therefore unnecessary for a Spiritualist healer healing through mediumship to concern themselves with the aura, otherwise those without physical sight would be rendered incapable of being healers, which would be a ridiculous state of affairs, as the etheric body, the pattern for life, is always perfect even when there are problems with the physical manifestation.

> "The spiritual self is a matrix of light which is mimicked by the aura which lies as a physical energy field..."

January 20 2001

Can you explain something of the plan behind Spirit communication?

The overall plan is to bring about what is so often called heaven on earth. To bring about joy without bound, boundless happiness generated by love which dispels all fear.

For when it is known that all are spirit and of the spirit, the manufacture of hateful things on earth will cease, and thus a more healing and natural environment will prevail.

The world of spirit and messengers from the Great Spirit seeks to allay all the worries with the earth plane so that the earthly physical experience is not marred by the blemishes from which it has almost always suffered until now.

At the beginning of human time, there was no real distinction between heaven and earth which is the fabled Garden of Eden scenario.

The plan is to return all of humankind, and in tow all the rest of creation, back to that Garden of Eden, but with greater understanding of the physical life's impact on the spirit and the spirit world.

January 27 2001

Why is it that we hear so much about a Spirit plan, and yet see such little apparent result of it?

We would point out that to the pessimist a glass of water is half empty, to the optimist it is half full.

There has been much progress in the awareness of the spiritual life of the human being on the earth plane since the middle of the 19th century of the common era.

There is no comparison to be made with primitive lifestyle and aspirations of early human beings and those who are currently inhabiting the physical in this 21st century.

Everywhere you look you will find a growing awareness of spirit life and life as spirit, and just as you would throw a small pebble into a very large pool and watch the ripples spread outward, so every communication from the spirit world to the incarnate world makes such an impression.

There is still much to be done, but much has been done in a relatively brief span of earthly time; and will be done. Thy will be done on earth and in heaven the same.

Amen.

February 3 2001

Why is it that automatic writing, of all psychic exercises, seems to be the least reliable? In whose opinion is writing given from good spirit individuals residing in the higher realms of light and love unreliable?

Automatic writing is exactly that. The person who is acting as a scribe for someone else in such a way that their own mental faculties are set to one side as it were, can only be propelling the fingers and chosen writing instrument across a page, therefore the resulting communication must be reliably from the spirit world, whether persons receiving the communications thus provided accept their content or not is entirely a matter of their own conscience and responsibility.

As in any mediumistic communication between the two worlds one has to guard against infiltration from the lower orders if one may call them such, perhaps the kindest description, but these mutterings when written are usually easily recognised. Other than that automatic writing is just that which it states itself to be. Only the content should be judged, even the spirit within the writer could be responsible for and influence the communication to the physically conscious earthly world.

February 10 2001

How Can Dreams Be Accounted For? Some Of Them Can Hardly Be Accepted As Memories Of Spirit Travels.

Quite true. The ability to dream is a necessity of human physical life. Dreams enable the subconscious to deal with the conscious problems that arise for the spirit during the physical conscious hours. If a human being is deprived of sleep, the dream state will kick in giving rise to hallucinatory conditions, this is a very dangerous situation for any human being to find themselves in.

Sleep deprivation leads to great mental distress. The change in consciousness which occurs in the life cycle of the human being when the conscious mind is asleep may be used in much the same way as it is utilised by those in the spirit realms during what is commonly known in mediumistic terms as trance.

In this changed consciousness the individual may receive impressions and communications conveyed from the spirit realms. There has been much documentation of this fact throughout the ages. Jacob's dream is a very famous one as is Elijah's.

Dreaming is part of the physiological process for those dwelling on the earth plane, but there is as always a spirit nonmaterial dimension at work too. May all your dreams be pleasant ones.

February 17 2001

Does the communicating spirit know whether he or she has registered on our consciousness in sleep state?

The consciousness that is referred to is not that of the physiological brain but that of the mind, which is of the etheric and spirit self, and as we have no intention of providing a map of the mind so that those with ill intent on the earth plane may devise the destruction of it in others, we can only tell you that from the spirit side of life and science.

It is known where to touch that consciousness in order to communicate between our two worlds, but we are not prepared to tell you where that point is, or how it may be found on the earthside.

Dreams themselves that contain images conjured up by the subconscious and the brain occasionally contain content emitted from the spirit realms and this activity is of course able to be detected on the physical plane.

It is therefore better to refer to the super consciousness in spirit communication practice. It is a little more difficult for the earthbound being in the physical state to identify specific spirit communication that occurs while they are without physical consciousness than it is to sort out the wheat from the chaff before milling flour.

"Everywhere you look you will find a growing awareness of spirit life and life as spirit, and just as you would throw a small pebble into a very large pool…"

February 24 2001

If a person is compelled to live a life of loneliness on this earth, is he or she compelled to lead that life after death?

There are very few instances of any human being being compelled to live their life in loneliness although there are individuals who falling foul of others or by circumstance who are so compelled.

The human being is a sociable animal by physical nature and ordinarily lives with a reasonable measure of comfort within a socially constructed framework with their fellows.

Others may feel a loneliness which would be assuaged by giving their love and service to others and by so doing come into contact with other human beings thus lessening their loneliness.

In this way too those who may be compelled perhaps by physical constraints to live a life of loneliness would be given an opportunity thereby for the easement of their condition through such easement of others' conditions being helped by those who are able to help themselves in this way.

We all are individuals in spirit as well as body and by definition we are alone, but seeking interaction with others we feel ourselves to be part of a group nevertheless. We are indeed all fractions of the whole even though life conditions may cause someone to have to live on their own or to otherwise feel deeply that they are alone. These only relate to the physical earth plane.

The world of spirit which even those who are so alone may have intercourse with is a truly gregarious place and no one spirit ever experiences spirit life alone.

There are exceptions but these do not concern those of a spiritual nature and who are in any case trying to live a reasonably ethical life on earth.

All have the company of those in spirit whatever their physical conditions.

May your lives be filled with service and love.

"Others may feel a loneliness which would be assuaged by giving their love and service to others..."

March 3 2001

I get very depressed with dogmas and organised religion. Yet I find some goodness in the church.

A religion in itself is an integral part of the need of human beings to structure their environment both physical and spiritual while living on the material side of life.

Therefore, many who think similarly have grouped themselves together, the common denominator of course being that desire to worship their Creator which we say is inbuilt and cannot be denied. In so worshipping the fount of their lives so it feeds the soul of the individual.

Spiritual sustenance for the majority of human beings needs to have a recognisable form such as is taken literally with what is called the communion wafer and wine, and even that practice is enveloped within a specifically designated framework, and this satisfies the soul for many.

The human being is compelled to attempt to bring order into the chaos that prevails on the earth plane, and by use of religious ritual, dogma and doctrinal practices seeks so to do.

There is much spiritual truth underlying much of what may appear to be somewhat shallow ceremonials on the surface of it, but those who understand the life of the spirit and the world of spirit, both here and there, are not critical of any grouping which feels that this is the way forward for its spiritual purpose.

Spiritualism is an all-pervading truth, but even it will not flourish as it should unless this need for a framework is understood and acted upon by all to whom Spiritualism is their religion.

As the primitive human being learned to use tools which could be used to build or destroy so humankind now has the tools of spirit which they must use wisely in constructing within the material and materialistic world the Spiritual edifice that is called Spiritualism, that it may admit the whole of the human race.

We wish you well in your endeavours. May the Great Spirit bless your task.

March 10 2001

If a child dies as a result of an accident, was that intended by the Great Spirit?

As much as human beings by reason of their very nature wish to know everything, they may not, and Good is not served by requiring only the answers to everything.

It has been stated many times before, but we will say it again that the intentions of the Great Spirit, Creator of the Universe will never be revealed to those living still on the earth plane in the natural animal condition but is only to be received when the Almighty so decides.

There may indeed be a perceived reason after any accidental event affecting the lives of those on the earth plane, but this is to do with the progression of the soul as it reaches out and back to the higher planes of life that are not of the gross animal material of which we have already made mention.

Those who appear as children may in reality have a spirit which is maturer than their apparent earthly years, the soul to which that spirit may belong may have existed before earthly time began.

Sorrow at the accidental physical death of a human being who seems not to have fulfilled the expected lifespan on the earth plane may later be found to be turned to a richness of deed and thought. Sorrow is best assuaged by service, service and more service to the world in which you find yourself, thus turning tragedy into triumph.

The will of that inimitable and unknowable source of all life prevails no matter what and that is not an accident.

May God bless all of you as little children. Amen.

"It has been stated many times before, but we will say it again that the intentions of the Great Spirit, Creator of the Universe will never be revealed to those living still on the earth plane..."

March 17 2001

Why are children born with defects, such as being crippled, through no fault of their own?

This is not a question of spirit. Physical handicap comes about as a result of problems within the material world.

They are nothing to do with the spirit impulse for the spirit pattern from which everything derives its physical form is always what would be accepted as the perfect result.

However, the material world is imperfect and the misfortunes that befall the physical body of the human being before it is born into the world of the earth plane are purely physical in origin.

It may be that there is some fault in the genetic material which has lain undiscovered or in any case may well have been overlooked and even ignored by any one on the earth plane whether medically qualified or not. The spirit is always of perfection.

The physical outward body of a human being because it is to the human being that you refer in your question has to be suffered and even those in the physical body that conforms to the norm will suffer in it.

There are of course degrees of physical suffering as in any other situation or condition.

No blame should be apportioned in the case of physical malformation or malfunction after birth into the physical world for it is a fact that the physical world has a dense and gross material.

Fortunately, the spirit will always rise above it, no matter what befalls it in the physical. The whole of earthly life is one of learning to put up with it and it is often felt that most progress is made by those who suffer the most.

May the knowledge of the love of the Great Spirit for all human creation bring comfort in the suffering of humanity. The flesh is indeed weak.

The spirit is always willing. God bless you all.

March 24 2001

How would you explain death to a child?

A child will not ask what is death for; it has no substance in a child's life because a child is so near to having come from that world of spirit to which all journey on during the earthly life before passing back into it.

A child may rather wonder about the mechanical aspects of why someone that they knew has stopped functioning. Why they may be laying on top of a table in the front parlour in a box rather than occupying a favourite chair by the fireside, and where there has been familiarity with the person; why there is no movement or response from the physical body of someone with which they come into contact whose spirit has passed over.

It is the adults around them who will inform the child that this condition of inertness is caused by death.

They may follow that according to their religious beliefs and convictions with more mystical and fairy-tale-like allusions to the whereabouts of the soul of this person who is now dead and physically entered a state of death.

It is most important therefore that the responsible adults answer any enquiry from a child as to what has happened when they come into contact with the condition of physical death, that the person actually has no more use tor their physical body. In the case of an old person, one might say that just like an overcoat or a school uniform it is has worn out or been outgrown by the person who has occupied it for such a long time.

In the case of the passing over of younger persons, while it may be fairly acceptable to say that they have been taken to be an angel, it is wiser to say that they themselves chose to go to the heavenly hosts, as otherwise a lot of resentment against the one who has taken the younger person can ensue, with negative implications for the recipient of that slightly erroneous communication. The child should be told that life is what should be of interest to them, and that the inanimate body is animated by our spirit which is part of the Great Spirit of all life that has no end; in this way, the emphasis is always on life and living.

It is the principles by which we live our lives that is most important, and this should be instilled as a matter of course into any child, including those who may be precocious enough to ask that vexed question, what is death?

May your lives be full of spiritual knowledge and may all your questions be answered eventually in the fullness of yours and our eternity. Amen!

March 31 2001

When people pass on, are there spirit doctors to care for them, both before the event and after it?

A doctor is an individual who is qualified in a particular science and area of knowledge. There are many qualified in the caring sense to attend to the business of doctoring to those who would seek their attention and ministrations.

You are asking of course about those who would be among the medical profession on the earth plane. Rightly they are given earth plane appellations that appertain to earthly conditions such as physicians and surgeons.

Those who would tamper with the thought processes engendered by things other than produced by the physical brain and body are not referred to here.

To understand the needs of those who are in the process because of physical illness passing over in the spirit world and then arriving there - they are given every nourishment for their spirit that their character shaped by physical condition can allow to pass through to them as individuals.

There are personalities on the spirit side of life who were not qualified in the physical sense to be in a position of expertly doctoring to those in such need while they were on earth but who have evolved and learned and are now able to attend the suffering of those left on the earth plane.

This is a continuing situation. On certain levels of spiritual evolution you will find those who are deemed ministering angels.

It may not be fashionable now on the earth plane to refer to these doctors from spirit as such, but that is what they are.

In earthly life they may have occupied most menial station which would have no bearing on their capacity to help others who are suffering in a positive way, and this of course they proceed to do when they arrive on the other side of life.

We have said before and we will say it again, there are no earthly titles or even categories for those who dwell in the spirit realms. May we mention that this is often the seat of the problem when communication is affected between those on the spirit side of the veil.

It is easy to forget one's name in spiritual circumstances, particularly if one is part of a working group. The Almighty Creator has no name which is known.

Yes, there are therefore in your terms doctors from the spirit world who minister to the sick and suffering before they pass over, and yes there are doctors in loving attendance when those they have cared for before that passing join their loved ones and those who love them on that next stage in the life of the spirit within.

May we wish you who are receiving our communication every blessing in your life's journey for you and your families and friends on behalf of all those of spiritual and Spiritualist persuasion at this special time of the earthly year. May the Great Spirit bless all who work for enlightenment and the good prospect.

"The story of the Tower of Babel illustrates the difficulties on the earth of translating thought when wishing to converse one person with the other..."

April 7 2001

In the whole of history has the Great Spirit ever spoken without coming through a spirit entity?

In the beginning was the word. Speech is the translation of thought images. The universe and all that is within it, that has ever been, that is, and that will ever be, proclaims the voice of God.

You refer to the idea that the Great Spirit uses a sound vibration with which to communicate directly to those on the earth plane. The difficulty with that situation had it ever occurred in the way that it has been spoken of, is it a language of the usual kind was used to give meaning to that communication.

There is a universal language of spirit because it is transferred by thought imagery. The story of the Tower of Babel illustrates the difficulties on the earth plane of translating thought when wishing to converse one person with the other.

The Great Spirit spoke and the universe was created. Since then those in the spirit realms in the most high have brought sweet influence to bear in true duty to that Creator who speaks to us in all there is. Those who listen for the voice of God will never be disappointed.

God bless you all of that creation.

April 14 2001

What advice can you give to one who wishes to start a home circle?

First of all, the desire to convene a circle meeting at one's own home demonstrates a need for spiritual enlightenment for this is the real purpose of the home circle, far outweighing any considerations of the possibility of development of psychic abilities.

It is known that the honing of psychic attunements assists in the begetting and acquiring of mediumistic achievement, but the home circle is very special. The circle may consist of only two spiritually motivated people, or more may be drawn to join in. As the home circle is always guided by spirit helpers, so the thought of that home circle coming into existence will be noted and acted upon so that individuals mostly of a spiritual nature will be guided towards that organiser.

If it is considered in the spirit realms to be suitable, then sitters for the home circle will be found.

The home circle has produced some of the Spiritualist movement's most illustrious exponents of the teachings from the higher realms as well, it must be admitted, as those who grace the public platform and bring evidential proof of survival to the gathered masses.

We wish all well who embark on this plan of action in the service of spiritual truth.

Can you explain something of the plan that is behind the spirit communications?

Communication between the spirit world and the world of matter was commenced at the beginning of earthly time.

The plan is the same now as it was then to bring a heavenly influence to bear on the life of the earth particularly for the human being who has been given responsibility for its welfare.

In the last hundred and fifty-three years there has been an upsurge in the acknowledgement by the ordinary person of the reality of the spirit. This is slowly and painfully being brought to the consciousness of all who inhabit the earth.

The plan is not for a Utopian dilettante existence for physical beings but to bring the two worlds manifestly closer together for the spiritual benefit of all - to bring the knowledge which is the true light of God - which is understanding.

April 21 2001

Is the spirit world planning a further revelation by sending another teacher like Jesus?

Since the beginning of time there has been expectation that one who will save the world and all its inhabitants shall visit from the realm of the One Most High.

There have been on occasion individual entities from the world of spirit who have come and indeed are messengers from the Great Source, but so far none have excited or changed the lives of so many for the better than the one called Jesus.

There are plans to send another such as he was and is, but humankind will have to remedy its ills in a more positive way before those who reside in the brightest light of all should send another - every time a human being is crucified by the inhumanity of others, an occurrence which is continual and has been continuous since the beginning of time, it will be of no use for such a one to walk the earth again.

The gospel of love is still of the utmost importance for humankind and until the problems of conditions which are unloving are remedied only then would the kingdom of God attempt by direct means to establish itself on the earth plane.

The human race must continue to better its lamentable record and begin to love each other as they were once directed, but we leave you with love and hope. The time will come.

"The plan is the same now as it was then to bring a heavenly influence to bear on the life of the earth particularly for the human being..."

April 28 2001

Do spirit laws work in the same way in your world as they do in this?

There is only one spirit law and that is the law of equilibrium, the law that is everything in harmony with the universe, both material and etheric, solid and spiritual. The law that is operating all that is, that was, and that will ever be, is the law of perfect harmony.

Love is the perfect vibration through which pervades harmony reaching out to everything that exists in the material world and in the world of the spirit. We do not speak here of the multitude of ways in which love expresses itself because there are instances of the abuse of the concept of love.

Therefore, it is best to consider harmony as the supreme spirit law. The striving for that harmony is what the soul's progress is all about, working towards harmony with the Great Spirit that is all-pervading and all-encompassing that all may dwell in the light of that spirit law for eternity.

Harmony seeks constantly to negate evil, to bring the patently bad into a realisation of good, to become harmonious is the ambition of those who seek to dwell in peace and love.

There is harmony in the highest. There will he harmony eventually amongst even the lowest orders of life. It has been said that you must judge yourself before you are judged - for the attainment of harmony you must judge and rectify yourself to find a harmony within, and link with the harmony without.

"Therefore, it is best to consider harmony as the supreme spirit law. The striving for that harmony is what the soul's progress is all about..."

May 5 2001

Do all paths lead to God; the same place?

All may approach God who so wish. The paths to God are many and various, but they all have one thing in common and that is a determination to do the best they can in every circumstance by those who would walk the path of God.

As long as there is a purity of heart and good intention on the part of those who walk their particular pathway to God, they will reach their goal in the end.

Those who fall by the wayside on what might be called their pilgrimage will find themselves lifted up and helped back on to their pathway, and they in their turn will then be able to stoop to pick up others who have fallen by the wayside.

All pathways to God are signposted with acts of service and kindness. There are many staging posts where those on their own pathway to the Source Of All Creation may rest awhile in their travels, take stock of their own progress, making good that which is bad within themselves in order to continue onward with a renewed determination, energy and hope.

There are paths which lead away from God, but even these eventually will turn back on themselves even against the wishes of the travellers who walk these unpleasant paths to lead them back towards God.

The light of the Great Spirit illumines every soul's pathway. It is up to the individual to allow that light of goodness into their lives in every way so that they are assured that their pathway will lead them to God.

Those who try to feel their way and shut out that illumination from the Most High are in need of the prayerful thoughts of what are after all their fellow travellers who are all ultimately going in the same direction to arrive perhaps sooner than those who take the paths of digression.

Those who follow a spiritual pathway and do no harm, are all on pathways to God, no matter what ceremonial or religious belief system they adhere to whilst on the earth plane.

It was once said that all roads lead to Rome, well we say that all roads lead to God. May God, the Great Spirit, bless your journeys all.

"Those who follow a spiritual pathway and do no harm, are all on pathways to God..."

May 12 2001

'In the Spirit life, do we join again with those we love and become younger?

Jesus says there is no marriage or giving in marriage. Where there is love which has its basis in the pure spiritual concept of unconditionality, so those who so love each other shall beyond doubt rejoin each other in their continuation in spirit.

Of course there is no marriage which is a social invention and has at its root economic benefit, and Jesus lived his earthly life within customs that even now would appear non-egalitarian where a woman would indeed be given without her particular consent in a marriage arrangement to another family. Sometimes of course the marriage would be allowed within the same family as first cousins for instance.

Jesus's teaching evoked kindness and fairness and he would not have concurred with the contracting of the marriage state as it was in his times. It is not surprising therefore that he himself did not enter into any such marriage. The voluntary marriage between persons of a mature earthly age. And holding great love, respect and consideration for each other, is however to be extolled, and should the minds and spirits of those so joined in their earthly lives be of a proper nature then of course they will be reunited in the world of spirit after their passing.

The world of spirit has no convention of physical monogamy, being purely of the spirit, therefore those of deep love having spent time on the earth plane with more than one partner may equally meet up once again with those they love on the other side. Spiritual love knows no age, nor gender.

It is part of the divine pattern of love which is eternal and therefore never dies.

"Jesus's teaching evoked kindness and fairness..."

May 19 2001

Would it not be best for all healers to be in perfect health themselves before they begin to heal others?

The most important aspect of health is a healthy spirit within the body of the physical material. Spiritual health is of most importance to humanity at large.

It is a popular belief that wrongdoing has a reverberating effect on the physical body, but this is only as far as the natural physical laws are concerned, such as the ravages that show on the face of a human being who lives a life of physical debauchery.

Even the physically debauched human being may have an innate spirituality which saves them from spirit disablement. Of course those who try to live a good physical life are not spared illness or accident any more than those who are at least outwardly deemed to be of bad condition.

Those who would give healing should be aware of their own spirit, and strive for the best in themselves, so that their spirit is strong, and the suffering that they have also endured in the physical life is put to good use in the service of bringing ease and comfort to the spirit within, and therefore to the physical condition of those who seek healing from them.

Many healers would not be as efficacious in their ministries had they not themselves experienced the sometimes hidden joys of their own weaknesses, and although this seems to be a flippant remark, it is serious, for there is a joy and a blessing to be found in human suffering because it is on the stepping stones of overcoming difficulties that the soul eventually ascendeth. We wish you all good health.

"Those who would give healing should be aware of their own spirit, and strive for the best in themselves..."

May 26 2001

Mediums - must they be born or can they be trained?

We are all born mediums for we receive information through the bodily senses and respond to our environment accordingly.

In the Spiritualistic sense, the more hidden ability, that of psychic reception and transmission, is also inherent in all who are born; but like every other gift from the Creator, some seem to have more quantity of talent accompanying the gifts than others; but all mediumistic abilities should be given the opportunity to develop within a suitable structuring and framework, for without the discipline and application of others' knowledge of the subject, those who would use their mediumistic faculties would be rather like pollen blowing on the wind, and would be reliant on chance to bring their mediumship into bloom.

For as pollen requires certain actions to propagate the bloom so certain action is required to produce such fruits of the spirit.

The passing on of knowledge is a wonderful and constructive occupation for established mediums, whether in this world or the other.

June 2 2001

What is the best way to achieve a perfect state of society?

The problem has always been for human beings that each individual has his or her own idea of what would constitute a perfect state of society.

However, the universal consensus of opinion throughout the ages has been that a perfect state of society is achieved by the understanding of each individual of what is the right and generous and loving system that operates from within the fair-minded and spiritual individual projecting those precepts into a social structure, that which is called the state of society.

There are many different factions who claim to know the answer to your question, but they may not address the real problems. If the underlying and underpinning principles of a sound, generous and beneficial to all society structure are put in place with love towards one's fellow beings, that would indeed be a social structure near perfection.

Spiritual values must prevail and only then can a good society flourish.

June 9 2001

Do you think laughter at seances is beneficial to results? Laughter as they say is the best medicine.

Feelings of happiness that are expressed by the expulsion of air through the larynx release stale air from the physical body and this has a beneficial effect on the physical being of the one who is laughing. The enjoyment of an innocent joke is beneficial to the psyche of the human being, and it is a way in which all present care may be forgotten for and during that occurrence. Seances themselves cover all meetings of groups of two or more sitting to receive communication from the spirit realms and a positive and happy atmosphere is sought for the best results. All such communications from good spirit require harmonious atmospherics in order to produce the best results.

Communication between the worlds is made on the frequencies that are set up by positive vibrations in the earthly atmosphere, and by atmosphere we are not referring to the mixture surrounding the planet earth only, but where the human being presently thinks that there is none.

Communication can be received inter-dimensionally throughout the physical universe without exception. We could say that it relies on those aspects of the human condition which are termed innocent happiness and laughter.

Where there is solemnity in the seance room let there be a suitable levity. Raise the spirits by raising your spirits. May the angelic hosts join in your laughter.

"A perfect state of society is achieved by the understanding of each individual of what is the right and generous and loving system that operates from within the fair-minded and spiritual individual..."

June 16 2001

Do spirit guides approve of cremation?

There is nothing to approve or disapprove in such a method of disposing of the dead carcass which is the physical body after the light of the spirit has left it.

There has been, and unfortunately still is, much superstition surrounding the processes of the physical transition into that other state of being. As the body rots so much rot is spoken about what should be done with it. Some would place the carcass in a pot and eat it. Some would place it on a high escarpment.

Others would bury it way beneath the ground on which they themselves move around in their physical forms. It is a shame that there is not as much understanding of the spirit dimension to life eternal as there should be, in spite of all the work that has been done to enlighten from the spirit realms.

In fact human beings themselves have sometimes wilfully tampered with messages on this subject in order to serve their own material purposes, whether this be to hold a group in subjection and thrall to a doctrine that they wish to impress on a subjective populace, or for outright material gain, as in the carrying out of the rites that they then associate with disposal of the physical body.

There is no secondary resurrection of the flesh. We who are of light, who live in the light, have no eventual need of the meat and bones of the physical existence. Only the rainbow of life prevails.

May the Great Spirit shed its light over all of us. All one in the light. Amen!

"It is a shame that there is not as much understanding of the spirit dimension to life eternal as there should be..."

June 23 2001

Is it necessary for a medium to be deeply entranced for a guide or control to come through?

It is time perhaps for the lexicography of Spiritualist practice and indeed spiritual practice to be revised. Entranced is not an appropriate term for the raising of the physical vibration in order to make contact with the other dimensions of life.

Entranced does refer to a rapturous state of mind which in everyday language would be applied to the feelings one might have for a beautiful picture or piece of music, not the hypnagogic state whereby the spirit world may transmit its communications to the plane of earth as it is still called.

There are many different levels of frequencies of mind used by spirit contact provided the medium is adept at closing down that part of their own consciousness that governs their own reason and emotion and imagination to the extent that they become a pure receiver and transmitter of communication, they do not have to render themselves or be rendered unconscious as in for instance the sleep state.

Every medium works in a different way. Each individual that makes up the whole of humanity is unique, and this uniqueness must be reflected in those who would demonstrate mediumship. No, it is not necessary for a medium to be deeply entranced.

The Great Spirit of Light and Love imbues all.

"Healing is always beneficial to those suffering from such mental and physical disarray..."

June 30 2001

Doctors say that some of the major sicknesses are due to pressure and business worries. In such cases how much does disharmony contribute?

Anxiety generates erratic mental and thereafter physical behaviour patterns, both within the bodily self of the individual so affected and outwardly manifesting. These aberrations from the harmonious norm create chaos in varying degree of the entire individual's system.

We would at this point counsel that symptoms of anxiety are not easily treatable by anyone whether it be the person so affected or a physician ministering. The causes of anxiety however are able to be addressed by the person who for instance identifying the cause themselves takes steps to remedy the problem.

In extremis some have been known to raise their hand against themselves, but it is better to change the root of the problem, for instance to cease the business one may be in or the situation generally if it contains the irritant factor, and to continue life on a different tack.

Healing is always beneficial to those suffering from such mental and physical disarray, but where distress is caused by the pressures of business, work, or home life, these issues still have to be addressed by the individual who is suffering.

Physical illness can be caused by stress, but it is better for the sufferer to relieve their symptoms by assessing and remedying the cause, than to expect doctors and surgeons to make good the manifestations that have occurred.

We wish you a harmonious and comforted and comfortable pathway in life.

"Physical illness can be caused by stress, but it is better for the sufferer to relieve their symptoms by assessing and remedying the cause..."

July 7 2001

Youth v Society

In speaking of the rebellion of the young against organised society, a questioner asked, "Do you agree that possibly they are much more attuned to the other world and are responding to guidance from it without knowing It?"

There are many sections of earthly society that we would wish would respond to guidance from the spirit realms.

So far this has largely only taken place with the use of individual intermediaries, within the confines of particular religious belief systems. Where youthful people gather within those religious systems or conclaves, there is usually much response to guidance.

However, the nature of youth itself is to be rebellious and to find fault with its elders and dare we say it mostly betters.

Where there is inequality of life conditions, injustice within the social system within which the youthful ones have to live, guidance is made available on an individual basis, and just as in Spiritualism and religious mediumship work, so some youthful ones are attuned more to the guidance which is always offered and is always present in the surroundings of earth, no matter how base the earthly condition, in order to make life and the living of it better for others of all ages.

Youth in the usual way of things becomes old age. May God bless human endeavours to make the world a better place.

"The nature of youth itself is to be rebellious and to find fault with its elders..."

July 14 2001

When dealing with the orthodox is it better to be gentle or harsh?

There are orthodox ways of dealing with situations in the various contexts of worldly life that are tried and tested and are efficacious. Even in the religious application some orthodoxy is very acceptable bearing in mind the nature of the human being and its leanings, propensity to weakness.

It is always better to treat fellow creatures with gentleness rather than make their lives on the earth plane any harder for them than they would be finding already; counselling is a gentle way of extrapolating the truth about someone else's ideas, particularly of the religious kind.

The orthodox religionist is only antagonised by harsh and abrasive criticism even if the philosophical thinker is putting forward what would be considered by evolved beings to be a rational argument against particular and narrowly defined religious orthodoxy.

Spiritualism seen as a religious definition supported by loving, acknowledged concepts for all who consider themselves to be cognisant of philosophical and scientific knowledge, could become a new religious bent whether orthodox or liberal. May all those who work for spiritual truth always deal as gently with others' ideas as they would have them deal with themselves.

July 21 2001

Will man survive?

The human being will survive in every sense of the word. From the beginning there was an inbuilt survival of both the physical as applied to the physical world, and of the illuminating spirit which is of course of the spirit world.

Extending this we look behind us at the long history of survival of the human race against all the odds. We look at the present and the difficulties which are presenting themselves to human beings and which they will survive, and then we look ahead into eternity, and perceive that scramble for physical survival prompted by the ever-surviving spirit - succeeding in conquering every obstacle that will ever be placed in its way.

It is not necessary to engage in conflict with itself as a race in order to effect that progress of which we speak. It is only necessary to engage the powers of construction and constructive thought in order to make good progress.

The endeavours of the human race to better itself are given great impetus by spiritual thought impulses generated both from the greater world of spirit and from within the soul of the individual human being.

Man, humankind, will survive, and eventually all will be well.

July 28 2001

To What extent does destiny play its part in man's earth life? Could you describe destiny? Is predestination an outside force or your own choice?

Human beings are generally born with self-will coming into the material world, equipped mostly to survive in it. This is achieved in the first instance by a constant selfishness, and as the human being matures, a self-centredness.

This is tempered by the spirit within and around, where there is a realisation of caring, compassion and consideration, in the world in which they find themselves, which of course includes their fellow human beings and other animate organisms such as the animals.

The substance of the planet upon which they tread and move amongst, is often not the object of those three C's.

There is a path that each human being is able to follow if they maintain that thread of spirit awareness throughout their earthly life.

The path is not singular, but is like a skein of wool, a bundle of paths that meet at various predetermined places in each life journey. These places are never missed which ever pathway the human being takes for itself.

It is not wise to attempt to divine too far ahead, because foreknowledge, too far in advance of events, may cause the traveller to take many a wrong turning before eventually ending up in the place they were supposed to be heading.

Our destiny is to be at one with All That is Good in the Light.

May you know that the Great Spirit is there and that all is a part of the Light. Amen.

"It is not necessary to engage in conflict with itself as a race in order to effect that progress of which we speak..."

August 4 2001

Perfection – can we attain it?

It was said that 'in the nature of the case, perfection cannot be attained because the question would be what happens after you attain it, when you reach the stage where you have nothing more to achieve?'

Perfection of a spiritual nature is where all aspects of consciousness attain a harmonious, balanced, yet knowing existence. It is the right thing for every individual to attempt to achieve this harmony and balance while they are in the earthly form, and to continue that striving onward into their spirit-only life on the other side of the veil.

Even by this striving so the vibrations of what is good and right will produce of itself a conducive situation for such harmony and balance to manifest within each one and other.

The concept of perfection is often made to appear an impossible goal, and even has scorn cast upon it and those who would attempt to achieve it in their lives. This to the detriment of all that is, in all the worlds, and all dimensions of life. Ultimate perfection is that achievement of harmony with the universe, both of matter and spirit, for the human being and its evolutionary progress.

The way in which the journey is undertaken is of utmost importance. To always search, within and without, for harmony and balance until it is found, then all will be as one with the Great Spirit.

"The path is not singular, but is like a skein of wool, a bundle of paths that meet at various predetermined places in each life journey..."

August 11 2001

How can one help another suffering from depression?

If the depression is being caused by problems with the environmental conditions or social conditions in which the sufferer finds themselves having to live, then it is obvious what the remedy should be.

The living conditions should always be as spiritually beneficial as possible.

If the depression is being caused by natural emotional responses to occurrences such as the breakdown of a past relationship, then that too may be remedied by recourse to a proper counsellor, who is well versed in such matters.

The remedying also applies to other such life disturbances that may cause the individual to feel depressed.

If referring to a clinically diagnosed condition, then that requires professional assistance at all times. It is possible now for sufferers from such depressive states to have their symptoms alleviated greatly by suitable medication, and this is the route that would be most advisable - a 21st century remedy for a 21st century malaise.

Spiritual healing is beneficial in every case of depression, no matter what the apparent cause.

A spiritual lifestyle can be adopted by any sufferer from depression to their better health both emotionally, mentally and physically. The physiology of the human being in the circumstances in which it now finds itself having to cope, is very pressured.

It is not surprising that there is so much depression, but with care, attention, love and kindness offered one to another, the human being will become uplifted of spirit.

All will be well.

"We wish all who offer themselves in this way our wish for their good health in every way and offer the blessings of the Great Spirit to all."

Printed in Great Britain
by Amazon